WORDS IN WORLD RELIGIONS

Peter D. Bishop

SCM PRESS LTD

334 01804 8

First published 1979
by SCM Press Ltd
58 Bloomsbury Street, London

Type set by Gloucester Typesetting Co. Ltd
and printed in Great Britain by
Richard Clay Ltd, Bungay, Suffolk

WORDS IN WORLD RELIGIONS

Contents

Preface

There has been a steady growth of interest in the study of the great
world religions in recent years, and many people are in need of help
with the vast body of information which an understanding of these
religions demands. Inevitably, the European who wishes to understand something of the history and practice of world religions must
come to terms with many words and expressions which will be
totally strange to him. It is impossible to speak of religions such as
Hinduism, Buddhism, and Islam without using words from the
original Sanskrit, or Pali, or Arabic. Few people will have had the
opportunity of studying these languages for themselves (although the
value of doing so in order to appreciate better the religion and culture
of which language is the vehicle should not be underestimated), but
they will need to understand technical words and to recognize the
significance of important names as they occur.

This book has arisen out of the practical need to help students in
higher education to understand the vocabulary of 'world religions'.
I have endeavoured to provide definitions and descriptions of the
most important words in six religious traditions. The book follows a
generally chronological order, and deals in turn with Hinduism,
Jainism, Buddhism, post-biblical Judaism, Islam, and Sikhism. This
arrangement accords with the way in which many courses in world
religions are taught and is intended to be helpful to students who will
wish to use the book for constant reference as they pursue studies in
the history of religions. It is also hoped that the book will provide a
useful introduction to the six religious traditions with which it deals.

An alphabetical index provides the means of locating words when
the chronological order is not appropriate.

At the end of each section there is a short bibliography. These
indicate the main sources I have used in compiling the sections and
is not meant to provide an exhaustive or up-to-date list of books for
further reading, although some of the titles will be useful for that
purpose.

I have to acknowledge generous help from a number of friends and
colleagues who have read parts of the manuscript and offered
comments and criticisms. For this I am indebted to Dr Kenneth
Cragg, of the University of Sussex, D. Howard Smith, lately of the

University of Manchester, D. A. T. Thomas, of the Open University, and Dr Michael Wadsworth, of Sidney Sussex College, Cambridge. It is hardly necessary to add that responsibility for mistakes which remain is entirely mine. I am also grateful to Miss Maureen Kelly, a post-graduate student at Sussex, 1977–78, for her help in the laborious task of compiling the index.

PETER D. BISHOP

Pronunciation

As an aid to pronunciation a few simple diacritical marks have been used. Their significance is as follows:

ā	as in cart	(In Rāma, the ā is pronounced as in farmer)
ī	as in sleep	(Sītā is pronounced See-taa)
ū	as in true	(In Rūpa, the ū is pronounced as in rhubarb)
ś	as in sheep	(Śiva is pronounced Shiva)
ç	as in cheap	(Brahmaçarya is pronounced Brahmacharya)

I The religion of the Hindus

Introduction

The religion that developed into the Hinduism we know today is complex and varied, and has developed over a period of about 4,000 years. During that time there have been born within the common cradle of Indian religion other forms of belief and practice which developed into the separate religions of Jainism, Buddhism, and Sikhism. Hinduism itself, however, never hardened into one form of religious expression and throughout its history it has continued to comprehend wide varieties of understanding, doctrine, devotion, and practice.

It is difficult to provide a concise definition of Hinduism, and it is important for the Westerner to realize how greatly it differs from the more familiar Christian religion. Hinduism can be defined in negatives. For example, there is nothing in Hinduism corresponding to a church; no single body of scriptures which is accepted by all the faithful as definitive; no creed to embody essential articles of faith. Even the word 'Hinduism' is a foreign invention. Hindus themselves prefer to describe their religion either by a phrase such as 'eternal truth' or by the particular loyalty or sect (Vaishnavite, Śaivite, etc.) which is their choice within the galaxy of Hinduism.

To obtain a positive definition of Hinduism one may begin by describing it as 'the religion of the Indian people'. This necessarily has to ignore the fact that among the Indian people there are also many million Muslims, Christians and Sikhs, as well as Parsees, Buddhists and Jews. Nevertheless, one can begin to define Hinduism by saying that it is the religion which has grown and flourished on the Indian subcontinent since at least 2000 BC.

Among the various forms of the religion there are certain basic beliefs and practices which Hindus hold in common. Socially, Hindus have been characterized by the practice of caste, by which all Hindus have been assigned a place in society, a community group with which to identify, and often an occupational pattern. Some of the most essential common beliefs of Hindus, such as karma and transmigration, are described below.

Karma

The word literally means 'work' or 'action'. Karma is the belief that every action has its consequences, good or bad, and that all bad actions must be compensated for by good deeds before salvation can be achieved. A person's karma is thought to accumulate during the course of many lives and to condition the state of life into which he is reborn. Karma thus provides an explanation for suffering and inequalities, for these may be attributed to behaviour during a previous life. The doctrine of karma is not confined to Hinduism. It is also found in Jainism and Buddhism.

Transmigration

Transmigration describes the belief that souls inhabit transient bodies; that at death the soul passes to a new body, either human or animal; and that the rebirth is conditioned by the karma accumulated in previous lives.

Samsāra

The continuous cycle of existence from which only liberation, or salvation, can free a person. The notion that history is represented by an ever-repeated cycle, rather than a linear progression, is typical of religions which arose in India.

Dharma

Dharma is an almost untranslatable Sanskrit word. It can mean a kind of cosmic order; a law, a way, or a principle; or the duty in life which is laid down for each individual.

Sanātana Dharma

Literally this means 'the eternal way', and is often used as a synonym for Hinduism.

Ārya Dharma

The dharma, or way, of the people of India.

2 Pre-Āryan and Āryan religion

One of the great river-valley civilizations of the ancient world was to be found along the course of the river Indus, in what is now Pakistan. The existence of this civilization had been suggested by occasional finds of statuettes and stamp-seals, but it was only in recent times (from the nineteen-twenties onwards) that archaeologists began to uncover the remains of a great city civilization and for the first time to provide direct evidence of the lives of the pre-Āryan people of India. Work still continues on the sites, and fresh material is being found, but we now know enough to appreciate the achievements of the remarkable people who lived in the Indus Valley in the third millennium BC.

The two main sites of excavation are at Harappā, one hundred miles south-west of Lahore, and Mohenjo Daro, two hundred miles north of Karachi on the Indus. The cities were extensive, with an area of about one square mile and in the case of Harappā an area of influence which is judged to have extended one thousand miles from north to south. The remains of the cities provide evidence of careful and centralized planning. The streets were broad and straight; the houses were built of brick, and were similar in design and construction throughout the area; and new houses had been constructed which were replicas of earlier buildings on the same sites. The houses were remarkable for their time, and show how advanced the civilization was. The larger houses were two-storeyed buildings with several rooms, including a bathroom. A drainage system carried water and waste away into covered drains in the streets. There were also rows of small terraced dwellings which are assumed to have been the living-quarters of manual workers.

To the west of each of the large sites were citadels, suggesting the necessity of defence against intruders from the mountain passes of the north-west.

One of the many interesting discoveries at Mohenjo Daro is a construction which has become known as 'the great bath'. It was an oblong pool, with small cubicles around the sides. Archaeologists believe, not that the swimming pool was in vogue in the Indus Valley before 2000 BC, but that this pool was used for ritual bathing, and that the small rooms around the sides may have been the living-quarters of priests.

The people of the Indus Valley were agriculturalists, growing wheat, barley and cotton, and keeping cattle, goats and sheep. The discovery of many crudely finished statuettes of female figures, with disproportionately large breasts and hips, suggests a concern for fertility, and perhaps the worship of fertility goddesses.

The digs revealed large numbers of stamp seals, which would have been used by the citizens to make their signatures. The seals bear engravings, usually of animals but sometimes of gods and people, and inscriptions. Unfortunately the writing of this ancient people, in a script which has 270 characters, has not yet been deciphered.

Archaeological evidence reveals the remarkable form and beauty of the Indus Valley civilization, but it also indicates the nature of its destruction. There are indications that from 2000 BC a series of raids was carried out on the area. Villages were burned, and as life became less stable houses were divided into smaller living-quarters. Finally the great cities fell. The destruction of Harappā and Mohenjo Daro occurred sometime around 1600 – 1500 BC. It was accompanied, if not accomplished, by fire.

The invaders who destroyed a great civilization were an aggressive group of warriors known as the Āryans.

They were a semi-nomadic people who originated in the area between the southern Russian steppes and the Caspian Sea. Around 2000 BC the Āryans began to migrate, some heading west to Greece and Italy (the farthest west that traces of the Āryans can be found is in Eire), some entering Persia (its other name, Iran, derives from Āryan) and some travelling south-east into India.

The Āryans had tamed horses and harnessed them to light chariots. With the mobility and striking power that these chariots gave them they were a formidable foe. They vanquished the cultivated city-dwellers of the Indus Valley and gradually extended their control further eastwards across the country.

Our knowledge of the Āryans comes mostly from their sacred literature, the Vedas. Like many other ancient writings the Vedas existed for a long time as an orally transmitted tradition before being committed to writing. The Āryan language was an early form of Sanskrit, from which most of the languages of northern India derive, and it has many direct links with other languages of the Indo-European peoples – Persian, Latin, Greek, and German.

The religion of the Rig Veda is clearly different from that of later Hinduism. The Āryans worshipped gods who were personifications of natural forces, regarded sacrifice as of paramount importance, and displayed no evident interest in the subtle reflexive thought which is found in later Indian religion. It would seem that the religious concerns of the Indus Valley people faded from view during the early Āryan period, only to reappear later. It is possible that the cultivated people of the land eventually won a victory of thought over their conquerors as the old and new religions were assimilated to each other.

Harappā
Mohenjo Daro

Cities of the pre-Āryan civilization of the Indus Valley, the remains of which were revealed by archaeologists from the 1920s onwards. The remains unearthed establish the existence of a remarkable civilization existing along the Indus Valley from about 3000 BC to the middle of the second millennium BC.

Stamp seals

The discovery of small seals had provided a clue to the existence of the Harappā culture before the archaeologists had discovered the remains of the cities. Digging at the sites led to the discovery of large numbers of seals which are thought to have been the identity discs of individuals. The seals are engraved with figures of animals and in some cases of gods and humans. The seals also bear inscriptions, but the language has not yet been deciphered.

Figurines

Many small statues have been discovered at these sites. They are fairly crudely made, and are often of women, emphasizing the maternal aspects of womanhood. One unusual figure more carefully formed than most is a bronze of a young girl, naked but for a necklace and bangles, and with a slim, boyish figure. The excavations also unearthed many pieces of jewellery.

Paśupati

Lit. 'Lord of the beasts'. Seals discovered in the Indus Valley show an image of a male god, wearing a horned headdress, sitting in a crossed-legged posture, and surrounded by animals. It is suggested that this 'Lord of the beasts' may have been a kind of prototype Śiva. In later Hinduism Śiva was regarded, among other things, as the patron of reproduction in men, animals, and plants, and in this role was known as Paśupati.

Linga

Among the discoveries at Harappā and Mohenjo Daro were a number of simple stone or metal pillars apparently representing the male generative organ. Later Hindu worship included the adoration of Śiva in the form of the Linga, which would be decorated with flowers or ghee. The Āryans at first reacted against this kind of worship, but it re-appears in later Hinduism.

Nandi

A humped-back bull, traditionally the mount of Śiva. Representations of a bull similar to Nandi are found on figurines of the Indus valley.

Dāsas
Dasyus

The term used by the Āryans to describe the conquered people of the land, and other earlier people of North-West India. Skeletal remains found at Harappā and Mohenjo Daro suggest that the early inhabitants included a group of Proto-Australoid type, with flat noses and thick lips, related to Australian Aborigines and some of the hill-tribes of India. But larger groups of people had features of a Mediterranean type, who may themselves have been earlier invaders.

Dravidian

The inhabitants of South India. The South Indian languages of Tamil, Telegu, Kannada and Malayalam are Dravidian languages and are quite different from the languages of North India, most of which derive from Sanskrit. A suggestion sometimes made is that the people of the Indus Valley fled south before the invading Āryans and became the ancestors of the modern Dravidians of South India. Whilst some movement of this kind may have taken place, it seems unlikely that such a simple explanation can satisfy all the known facts.

Āryan

The name given to the Indo-European invaders of India. They were part of a large group which lived between the Russian steppes and the Caspian Sea. Around 2000 BC they began to migrate, some travelling westwards to Greece and Italy (and some say as far west as Ireland), and others entering India. There are many connections between the language of the Indian Āryans (an early form of Sanskrit) and Latin, Greek, and Persian. The word 'Āryan' is from the same root as 'Iran', and some aspects of Āryan religion are similar to the Zoroastrianism of Iran.

Veda

The most ancient of the Indian scriptures. The earlier Vedas were the religious poems and instructions of the Āryans. The word is from the same root as the Greek *oida*, meaning 'I know'. The Vedas were preserved and handed down as an oral tradition for a long period before being committed to writing.

Rig Veda

The most important of the Vedas, consisting chiefly of hymns to the great gods of the Āryans. The gods are personified forms of natural forces. Sacrifice is an important element of the religion of the Rig Veda.

Sāma Veda

Collections of verses taken from the Rig Veda, but with their order rearranged, for use in chanting at the sacrifices. The verses are addressed chiefly to Soma, Indra, and Agni.

Yajur Veda

Prose utterances, consisting of instructions for use at the sacrifices, and concentrating upon ritual acts rather than upon the gods.

Atharva Veda

The Atharvas were a group of priest-magicians, and the Atharva Veda consists of versified spells for curing diseases. It is thought to contain much pre-Āryan tradition.

Brāhmanas

Also part of the Vedas, but composed considerably later than the Rig Veda. The Brāhmanas contain instructions concerning sacrificial ceremonies and prayers for the priests. There is little of religious interest in them.

Āranyaka

Lit. 'forest treatise': commentaries added to the Brāhmanas for the use of forest hermits.

Samhitā

Verses of a like kind; portions of the Vedas arranged according to subject.

Mantra

Collection of sacred verses from the Vedas. The word later came to refer generally to a verse which a guru taught to his pupil; sometimes the verses were thought to convey spiritual power upon the person who recited them. The most famous is the Gāyatrī Mantra, found in the Rig Veda 111.62.10.

Śruti

What is revealed. The Vedas, including the Vedanta, are regarded as revealed scripture, and so of special importance.

Smriti

What is remembered. Religious literature after the Upanishads is 'smriti', and so theoretically of lesser importance than śruti. But in practice some of the writings included under 'smriti' are of great significance and very influential (for example, the Bhagavad Gītā).

Varna

Lit. 'colour'; but the word also refers to the division of society into four main classes, a process which had already taken place at the time of the Rig Veda. From this division there developed thousands of caste groups, most of which related to occupation.

Jāti

Social status in a caste group determined by birth.

Brāhmin (Brāhman)

The highest of the four varnas, or broad caste groups, mentioned in the Rig Veda. The Brāhmins are the priests. Because of the immense importance attached to sacrifice, the Brāhmin's role in society was regarded as of first importance.

Kshatriya

The second of the caste groups, consisting of the warriors and rulers. At later periods in Indian history the Kshatriyas did include some notable spiritual leaders, the greatest of whom was Lord Buddha.

Vaiśya

The merchants, who constituted the third caste group.

Śudra

Menials or labourers. The lowest group in the caste structure introduced by the Āryans, although the Untouchables, who had no caste status, formed an even lower strata of society. Members of the lowest group may have been drawn originally from the conquered people of the Indus valley.

Dvija

Twice born. The three highest groups (Brāhmin, Kshatriya and Vaiśva) underwent the 'rebirth' of initiation, and were the only ones to have the benefits of religion fully available to them.

Purusha Sūkta

The 'hymn of man' in the Rig Veda which contains the first reference to varna.

Rāja

A ruler of an Āryan tribe, and later the Hindu equivalent of 'king'. The word relates to the Latin 'Rex'.

Sabhā
Samiti

Tribal councils which shared responsibility and power with the Rāja. The distinction between Sabhā and Samiti in Vedic times is not clear. The word 'sabhā' is commonly used of councils today, including that of the Indian Parliament.

Purohita

A chief priest of an Āryan tribe.

Grāma

Among the Āryans, this referred to a group of related families. Later the word simply means a village.

Rita

Truth, reality, or cosmic order, which the Āryans believed to be maintained by sacrifice.

Gods of the Rig Veda

Indra

The god of war and storm, and the most important god in the Rig Veda. Over two hundred hymns are addressed to him. Indra is a god in the image of the Āryan warrior, and the defeat of the people of the Indus Valley is sometimes attributed to him. His popularity later declined, and he is not an important god in later Hinduism.

Varuna

The sky. An important god in the Rig Veda, he largely disappeared in later Hinduism. There are possible connections between Varuna and Ahura Mazda, the Iranian god. As the sky god, Varuna sees all, and so has a strong moral role.

Rudra

A mountain god, who is sometimes described as 'the terrible', or 'the red one'. Rudra is a god of destruction, yet is also associated with the healing herbs of the mountains. He is the father of the Maruts. Rudra is possibly a forerunner of Śiva.

Maruts

Storm gods, especially associated with the mountains.

Agni

Fire. Agni is one of the most important gods of the Rig Veda. As the sacrificial fire, Agni mediates between men and the gods, and is essential to the maintenance of religion and order.

Soma

Drink of the gods and a god; a plant which was either a drug or an intoxicating drink. Soma was the drink of Indra, and so associated with the life-style of the Āryan warriors.

Vāyu

The wind. Although not very significant after the Vedic period, Vāyu was seen in a later Vaishnavite system as a mediator between God and men.

Usha

The dawn, and daughter of the sun. Many gentle and beautiful hymns are addressed to Usha, who is eternally young, beautiful, and beneficent. There are parallels to Usha in Greek and Roman religion.

Sūriya (Sūrya)

The sun. An important god in the Rig Veda. He is the 'eye of Varuna'. Sūriya is sometimes known as Vivasvat (brilliant, shining), a name which suggests a connection with the Zoroastrian Vivahant. Later sun-worship in India produced some famous temples, such as the Konārak temple, but solar temples were often associated with such perverse practices as temple prostitution.

Yama

Death. Yama passes judgment on the dead, whose good and evil deeds are recounted before him. The good are then sent to one of a number of heavens, and the bad to hell. This is an element of Indian religion which faded in later times with the development of the idea of samsāra.

Later trilogy of the greatest gods in Hinduism

Brahmā (Brahman)

The creator, who later came to be thought of not as a personal god, but as 'ultimate reality'. It is very rare to find a temple dedicated to Brahman.

Vishnu

The preserver of life. Vishnu does appear in the Rig Veda as a minor god. He is regarded by some as a god of the Indus Valley people who came to be of great importance as the Āryans were absorbed into the population. To Vaishnavites, he is the greatest of all gods. Around Vishnu there has grown up the avatāra doctrine, by which Vishnu is thought to be incarnated in a series of animals and people, some of whom are of great importance in popular devotion.

Śiva

The destroyer, although Śiva also has a beneficent aspect. In his destructive aspect, Śiva is associated with the fierce consorts, Durgā and Kālī. But after destruction, Śiva is thought of as re-creating, and so the common image of Śiva as Natarājan, or Lord of the Dance, expresses his creative power. To the Śaivites, Śiva expresses a concept of a personal, loving God.

Vishnu and Śiva became the great personal gods of devotional Hinduism. Most Indian temples are dedicated to one of them, or to their consorts or avatāras.

3 The Upanishads

Apart from scattered archaeological remains, the evidence for the development of Hinduism in its early period is to be found in its written scriptures. After the Vedas, the next group of scriptures to be formulated were called the Upanishads. The Upanishads contain a considerable range of material, written over a long period. Most were probably written between 800 BC and 300 BC, although it is likely that further additions were made to the Upanishadic writings after 300 BC. Some of the early Upanishads, written in prose and often in dialogue form, are generally agreed to date from before the rise of Buddhism in the sixth century BC.

The word 'Upanishad' is a composite word meaning 'sitting down beside'. It suggests the picture of a pupil sitting beside his teacher, or guru, in order to learn spiritual wisdom. Much of the dialogue of the early Upanishads purports to be instruction by the teacher and questions from the pupil.

The Upanishads are traditionally regarded as the last of the Vedic scriptures, bringing to an end the period of revelation, or śruti. So they are known as Vedānta, 'the end of the Vedas'. They constitute a reflection upon some of the questions which arose in the later Vedic period and deal philosophically rather than practically with them.

But the Upanishads are not simply a reflective conclusion to the Vedas. In some ways they reveal a considerable change from the earlier scriptures. For example, it is in the Upanishads that the ideas of karma and transmigration are first encountered. These basic concepts of Hinduism do not appear in earlier writings, yet the Upanishads appear to regard them as accepted truth. The introduction of such important ideas at the stage of Indian history represented by the Upanishads is therefore something of a puzzle. Were these concepts present in earlier times without reference ever being made to them? This seems most unlikely. Are the Upanishads more than simply a finale to Vedic teaching? This is much more probable. The likely answer is that the Upanishads represent change as well as development, and that by the time they came to be written ideas long subdued by the lively religion of the conquering Āryans had re-emerged and begun to coalesce with Vedic religion. The eastward movement of Āryan culture, towards Bengal, may also have provided opportunities for the introduction of new ideas from the local people.

Certainly a direct reading of the Upanishads conveys the sense of a very different approach to religion and life from that of the Rig Veda. In place of the concern with gods who represent natural forces and with the practice of sacrifice the Upanishads provide a picture of a deeply reflective approach to religion. They are much concerned with the relationship between the individual soul and ultimate reality, with the manner by which the ineffable Absolute may be mediated to the world of men and women, and with the deceptions of the phenomenal world which conceal spiritual truth from us. In matters of practical living they lend support to a style of life which aims eventually at a detachment from worldly concerns in order to find liberation from the oppressive cycle of rebirths.

The Upanishads are the most philosophical of Hindu religious writings, and they have provided a continuing source of reference for scholars and intellectuals. The main philosophical schools of Hinduism look to them for authority and inspiration.

The Upanishads

Tradition asserts that there is a total of 108 Upanishads, although it is most probable that a greater number have been written and circulated at various times, and there may have been as many as 200 in all. But only a few of the Upanishads have been in constant use and have served as the texts of philosophical schools.

Opinion varies as to how many 'principal' Upanishads there are. Figures of ten, thirteen, or fourteen are given by different authorities. The more important Upanishads include the following:

Aitareya	Mahānārāyana
Brihadāranyaka	Maitri
Chāndogya	Māndūkya
Īśa	Mundaka
Kauśītaki	Praśna
Kena	Śvetāśvatara
Ketha	Taittirīya

Śankara wrote commentaries on eleven of the Upanishads, the Aitareya, Brihadāranyaka, Chāndogya, Īśa, Kena, Ketha, Māndūkya, Praśna, Śvetāśvatara, and Taittirīya, and he made reference to the Kauśītaki and the Mahānārāyana.

The earlier Upanishads, including the Chāndogya and Brihadāranyaka, are in prose, and are generally held to date from before the rise of Buddhism in the sixth century BC. They are often in dialogue form, and deal with major philosophical ideas.

The later Upanishads, including the Ketha and Śvetāśvatara, are written in verse. In the later Upanishads there develop more personal concepts of God expressed through the notion of Īśa or Īshvara.

Ātman

The self. The word also means 'breath', 'soul' and 'life'. The Upanishads expound the view of a soul or self which inhabits successive bodies and does not perish with the death of the body. The Ātman is thus the imperishable element in man which migrates from body to body through the long cycle of existence. 'Ātman' is also used for the universal soul. In the Upanishads it is taught that Ātman the personal self, is to be identified with Brahman, the Absolute. When a person recognizes the identity of his own self with Brahman he becomes free from the cycle of transmigration.

Brahman

Ultimate Reality or the Absolute. A basic idea of the Upanishads is that Brahman is to be found in all existence, and that to recognize the presence of Brahman in all things and all people is to be close to the final truth which will ensure salvation. Especially important is the recognition that the individual soul (Ātman) is to be identified with Brahman and that the experience, rather than just the intellectual acknowledgment, of this truth leads to freedom. This use of the word 'Brahman' is to be distinguished from the term for the highest class in Hindu society, which is often spelled 'Brāhmin' to make the distinction clear. Brahman is the neuter form of the masculine Brahmā (see p. 10).

Māyā

Deception, illusion, or trick. The Upanishads suggest that the true nature of reality is concealed from us by Māyā, which leads us to suppose that the phenomenal world is all that there is, and blinds us to the reality of Brahman.

Nāmarūpa

Literally 'name-form', the term describes the world of phenomenal things which by the action of Māyā is made to appear as though it were all that is.

Moksha

Salvation or liberation. Moksha involves a release from the cycle of rebirths which can be obtained through knowledge, right action, or devotion to God.

Mukti

Like Moksha, Mukti is from a root which means 'to set free, let loose from', and is also used to describe the goal of liberation.

Avidyā

The word means lack of knowledge, or ignorance, and is used to express the idea that the cause of man's bondage to the phenomenal world is not wilful sin, but a lack of true knowledge.

The positive form, Vidyā, means knowledge, learning, or science, but especially knowledge of the Vedas, which comes from the same root.

Vedānta

Literally 'the end of the Vedas', Vedānta refers to the scriptures, especially the Upanishads, which mark the end of the Vedic period. They are 'the end of the Vedas' both in the sense that they complete the teaching of the Vedas and in the sense that they bring to an end the period of revelation (śruti) of the Vedas. The word is also used on occasion to describe one of the six main systems of Indian philosophy, although 'Advaita Vedānta' is a more accurate description.

Advaita

Advaita means 'non-dual', and is used of the philosophical system which teaches that only Brahman, or the Absolute, is entirely real. All else is illusory or transient. Brahman is in all things and all things in Brahman.

Brāhmanism

Hinduism of the period of the Upanishads and immediately afterwards is sometimes referred to as 'Brāhmanism' because of the dominance of the Brāhmin in the religious practices of the time. There was a revival of Brāhmanism in the early centuries of the Christian Era (CE) which may have been in part a reaction against the influence of Buddhism. The revival was marked by an emphasis upon the use of Sanskrit, hostility towards non-Hindu systems of thought or religion, and vigorous attempts to assert the supremacy of the Brāhmin class.

Saguna Brahman

Brahman with attributes. The phrase expresses the notion that there are three positive attributes that can be predicated of Brahman, and that they are existence, consciousness and bliss (in Sanskrit, Sat, Chit, and Ānanda).

Nirguna Brahman

Brahman without attributes. The contrary view which maintains that nothing can be predicated of Brahman, since anything that is said of Brahman must be less than the truth. Brahman is always more than can be said or thought.

Īshvara

God as Creator and personal Being, in contrast to the impersonal Brahman. Īśa, 'Lord', is an alternative form of the same word.

Svayambhu

Self-existent, an attribute applied to Īshvara in the Īśa Upanishad, and expressing a similar idea to the Western notion of God as necessary being.

Sat

Existence. That which is genuine or real. There are connections between this word and satya, or truth. What is true is what really exists, as opposed to the deceptions or illusions which people often take for reality.

Chit

Consciousness, intellect, or mind.

Ānanda

Bliss or joy.

Tat tvam asi

An important phrase in the Upanishads, meaning 'you are that', and expressing the idea that the individual, or Ātman, is essentially the same as the universal Brahman.

Uddālaka

A famous rishi, or sage, who appears as a teacher in the Upanishads.

Śvetaketu

The son of Uddālaka. In the Chāndogya Upanishad Uddālaka instructs his son in the nature of reality. Among a number of vivid images which he uses is that of the salt dissolved in water. The salt could not be seen, yet it could be tasted at the top, in the middle, and at the bottom of the container and so pervaded the whole. 'Here indeed in this body you do not perceive the true (Sat) my son, but there indeed it is. That which is the subtle essence in all that exists has its self. It is the True, it is the Self, and you, O Śvetaketu, are it' (Chāndogya Up. 6.13.2–3).

Yājnavalkya

A teacher and sage, and a character in the Upanishads. Yājnavalkya appears to be strongly critical of Brāhmanical tradition. Tradition ascribes to him the Yajur Veda, Śatapatha Brāhmana and Brihadāranyaka Upanishad.

Damyata	'Be self-controlled'
Datta	'Give'
Dayadhvam	'Be merciful'

These three great ethical qualities are taught in the Brihadāranyaka Upanishad in the form of a legend. Prajāpati repeated 'Da' three times (said to be an imitation of the sound of thunder). The three

'Das' were interpreted as Damyata, Datta, and Dayadhvam (Brihadāranyaka Up. 5.2).[1]

The Four Stages of Life

An ideal pattern of life suggested for the pious Hindu male in the Upanishads. It should be stressed that this is an ideal, and that few people would actually follow through all four stages in practice.

Brahmaçarya

The young man who goes to study as an apprentice in the house of his guru, or teacher. The student learns the scriptures and the values and traditions of his religion. Chastity is an important requirement of this stage of life.

Grihasthya

The married householder. Marriage and the begetting of children is regarded as an integral part of the religious life.

Vānaprasthya

The forest-dweller, who lives either alone or with like-minded companions. This stage marks a gradual withdrawal from the concerns of everyday life when the family is old enough to care for itself.

Sannyāsi

One who renounces. The final stage adopted by those who deliberately cut all the ties they possibly can with ordinary life in an attempt to attain liberation. The Sannyāsi renounces everything except a loincloth, a begging-bowl and a water pot.

4 The Epics

The Upanishads were suitable for the intellectuals, but they were not the kind of material to inspire ordinary people. For them the great

---

[1]This passage is referred to by T. S. Eliot in the last part of *The Waste Land*, 'What the Thunder Said', *Collected Poems* 1909–1962, Faber & Faber and Harcourt Brace, Jovanovich, New York 1963, pp. 78–9.

ideas of the Upanishads were conveyed by popular stories of heroes and saints and gods who embodied in their lives the central religious teaching of the time.

There were two great Epics in India, the Mahābhārata and the Rāmāyana. The stories they contain are still retold, acted out, and sung in villages throughout India. They provide inspiration and spiritual sustenance for millions of people, and are an important aid to the devotional religion which is characteristic of popular Hinduism.

The Mahābhārata was probably compiled by the third or second century BC and the Rāmāyana by the first century CE. Eventually the Epics were translated into the Dravidian languages of South India as well as into other Indian languages, and the appearance of these religious writings in local languages did much to spread a common Hindu tradition throughout the country.

The Epics do not have the same theoretical status as authoritative guides for the Hindus as do the Vedas. The Vedas are śruti, or revelation. The Epics belong to the class of literature designated smriti, or what is remembered. Yet for many ordinary people they are much more familiar guides to the religious and social teaching of the Hindus than the weightier matters of the Vedas and Vedānta. The Bhagavad Gītā, for example, which forms part of the Mahābhārata, is among the best known and most revered of Hindu scripture, in spite of its theoretical classification as smriti.

The Epics deal in larger-than-life stories in which kings, princes and princesses do marvellous deeds, demons of horrific form stalk the earth, and animals talk and fly. The fact that these tales contain so much that is clearly legendary or mythological is not taken by Hindus to be to their detriment. They recognize that here are spiritual truths conveyed through myth and fable, and they accept the Epics gladly on those terms. As one twentieth-century Hindu has written of the Epics,

> They are the records of the mind and spirit of our forefathers who cared for the good, ever so much more than for the pleasant and who saw more of the mystery of life than we can do in our interminable pursuit for petty and illusory achievements in the material plane . . .
> Mythology is an integral part of religion. It is as necessary for religion and national culture as the skin and the skeleton that preserve a fruit with its juice and taste. Form is no less essential than substance. We cannot squeeze religion and hope to bottle and keep the essence by itself. It would neither be very useful nor last very long. Mythology and holy figures are necessary for any great

culture to rest on its stable spiritual foundation and function as a life-giving inspiration and guide.[1]

Mahābhārata

The story of 'great Bhārata', the legendary ancestor of the Indian people (the name Bhārata is often used to indicate 'India'), and his descendants.

The Mahābhārata is a great epic, of about 100,000 stanzas. It grew over a period of time, and the first version of it was a mere 8,800 verses, with the title of 'Jaya', or victory. The original authorship is attributed to the sage Vyāsa. The main bulk of the Epic was completed by the third or second century BC, although it seems likely that some additions continued to be made until the second century CE. The earliest extant manuscript of the Mahābhārata is from the fifteenth century CE. It has been translated into all the main languages of India, as well as many other languages, and has become an important source of inspiration for bhakti religion. It puts many Hindu ideas into popular form, and stories from the Epic are read, sung and acted out as popular entertainment all over India.

The Bhāratas are mentioned in the Rig Veda as a martial people living in the area between the Ganges and the Yamuna rivers. It is probable that there is a genuine historical background to some of the Mahābhārata, although there has been much elaboration on this, with the addition of mythological and legendary material. The story is of a quarrel between two related groups, the Kauravas and the Pāndavas.

Dhritarāshta was the blind king of the Kauravas, or Kurus, but was not able to rule because of his disability. So his younger brother Pāndu was appointed king. Dhritarāshta had 100 sons, the eldest of whom was Duryodhana; Pāndu had five sons. After the death of Pāndu a quarrel broke out between the Kauravas and the Pāndus, which culminated in the great battle of Kurukshetra and the victory of the Pāndavas. The Mahābhārata teaches the importance of kingship and the values of duty and integrity. It fosters devotion to Krishna, who is presented as an avatāra of Lord Vishnu.

Rāmāyana

The other great epic of India, although a shorter work of some 24,000 stanzas. It is attributed to the sage Vālmīki. The present version was written in Sanskrit in the first or second century CE, although this was probably a rewriting of existing material. Although

---

[1]C. Rajagopalachari, *Ramayana*, Bharitya Vidya Bhavan, Bombay 1958, Preface to the 3rd edition.

compiled after the Mahābhārata, the incidents referred to in the Rāmāyana are thought to predate those of the larger epic by some 150 years.

The story of the Rāmāyana is in seven books, of which the first and seventh are regarded as late additions. It deals with the boyhood of Rāma, his marriage to Sītā, the withdrawal of Rāma and Sītā to the forest, the abduction of Sītā by the wicked Rāvana, the rescue of Sītā from the island of Śri Lanka and the return in triumph of Rāma to Ayodhyā.

The story, like that of the Mahābhārata, is very popular and a great disseminator of Hindu ideas and values among the ordinary people. It is much concerned with dharma, and with devotional religion. Rāma appears as an avatāra of Lord Vishnu, although many commentators regard that as a later embellishment of the earlier story. The Rāmāyana shows signs of Brāhmin influence, in the suggestions of an Āryan triumph over the people of South India and of Śri Lanka, and in a derogatory reference to the Buddha. Of the many translations of the Rāmāyana perhaps the best known is the Hindi version of Tulsī Dās.

Characters of the Mahābhārata

Dhritarāshtra

King of the Kauravas, or Kurus. Dhritarāshtra gained control of the kingdom, but custom prevented him from ruling because of his blindness. It was for this reason that his younger brother Pāndu became king.

Pāndu

The younger brother of Dhritarāshtra who became king in his brother's stead. The name 'Pāndu' means 'the light-skinned one', and some think that this suggests that the king contracted leprosy and for this reason had to leave his kingdom. Legend tells of his giving up the kingdom and retiring to the Himālayas because of a curse.

Yudhishthira

The eldest of the five Pāndava brothers. Hindu mythology represents him as the son of Dharma, and he is viewed as a model of integrity and justice. The reign of Yudhishthira was regarded as a golden age of prosperity, peace and righteousness. The one vice of Yudhishthira recalled in the legends was that of gambling. The Mahābhārata tells of a great dice-game between Yudhishthira and Śakuni, uncle of Duryodhana, in which Yudhishthira lost his kingdom to the Kauravas.

Arjuna

Another of the five brothers, and the most skilful warrior of them all. His skill won Princess Draupadī in a great contest at which the princess chose her husband. Arjuna is a principal character in the Bhagavad Gītā, in which his role as the leading warrior on the side of the Pāndavas provides the basis for the story of the Gītā. There are legendary tales of Arjuna fighting against the Dravidians in South India.

Bhīma

The second of the Pāndava brothers. His name means 'the terrible'. He was a great warrior with a fierce temper.

Nakula

The fourth of the brothers, but one who features little in the story.

Sahadeva

The youngest of the Pāndava brothers.

Draupadī

A beautiful princess who became the joint wife of the five Pāndava brothers. She was won by Arjuna's skill with her bow at the contest arranged to find her a husband. In the gambling match she was regarded as part of the Pāndavas' property to have been lost by Yudhishthira, and for a while she was the slave of Duryodhana. Draupadī had five sons, one by each of the brothers.

Drona

A teacher of military arts to the Kauravas and the Pāndavas. He was killed at the battle of Kurukshetra, in which he sided with the Kauravas.

Krishna

A leading character in the Mahābhārata. To him is attributed the Bhagavad Gītā, which forms part of the Epic; in the Gītā Krishna declares himself to be the Supreme Being.

The name Krishna means 'black', and artistic representations usually portray him as very dark skinned. The word 'Krishna' occurs in the Vedas, but there the reference appears to be to the dark-skinned people of the land conquered by the Āryans. It is possible that the Krishna of the legends was based upon an historical character, around whom later stories of divinity accumulated. The historical Krishna was said to be the leader of the Yādava people who lived by the river Yamuna, in the area between the modern cities of Delhi and Āgra.

Krishna came to be regarded as the eighth avatāra of Lord Vishnu, and one of the most popular gods of India. There are many stories of him in the Purānas, where he is portrayed as a mischievous boy and a lover who awoke uncontrollable passion in the cowgirls of Vrindāvana. Krishna became a focus for fervent devotional religion.

Nala and Damayantī

A king and queen whose story is included in the Mahābhārata. This story-within-a-story has been widely translated and is a well known part of the Epic. It is largely concerned with the perils of gambling (although not quite a moral tale against gambling, for Nala not only lost his beautiful wife and his kingdom in a gambling match but also regained them the same way). The story appears in the Mahābhārata as a tale told to Yudhishthira during the exile which followed upon his own gambling losses.

Characters of the Rāmāyana

Daśaratha

King of Ayodhyā, and a member of the Ikshvāku dynasty. Names of kings of this dynasty figure prominently in early inscriptions in South India, and this gives credence to the suggestion that part of the Rāmāyana, dealing with the battle against the 'demons' of Lanka, may reflect the conquest of South India by the northerners.

Rāma

The central character of the Rāmāyana. Rāma was a son of king Daśaratha. The story tells of his winning a beautiful wife, Sītā; of his being cheated of his proper inheritance on the death of his father; and of his being exiled to the forest with his wife and his brother Lakshmana. There the three were in conflict with the demons and their ruler, the wicked king of Śri Lanka. In a great battle Rāma defeated the king of Lanka and returned in triumph to Ayodhyā to enter into his inheritance. The years of his rule were said to have been a time of exceptional peace and stability, and the phrase 'Rām Rāj' is still used to refer to an ideal state of government.

Rāma is believed to be the seventh avatāra of Lord Vishnu in the Vaishnavite tradition, and as such is widely worshipped. His name, as Rām, is a common term for God.

Bhārata

The son of Daśaratha by his second wife, Kaikeyī, and so step-brother to Rāma. Kaikeyī tried to ensure that her son, and not Rāma, should succeed king Daśaratha. Only the integrity of Bhārata prevented this from happening. But during Rāma's exile Bhārata ruled in Ayodhyā as the regent of Rāma.

Lakshmana

The son of Daśaratha by another wife, Sumitrā. Lakshmana accompanied Rāma and Sītā on their wanderings in exile, and during the conflicts with the demons.

Śatrughna

The twin brother of Lakshmana, he plays a less important part in the Rāmāyana.

Sītā

The wife of Rāmā, and daughter of king Janaka. She voluntarily accompanied her husband into exile, and was captured by the demon king Rāvana and abducted to the island of Sri Lanka. Rescued by her husband and his allies, Sītā then had to undergo the ordeal of fire in order to prove that her purity had remained inviolate during her imprisonment. Although she was vindicated by the fire-god, Agni, Sītā's imprisonment became the subject of gossip, and she was banished from the court until her virtue was finally proved after a fifteen-year exile. Sītā is regarded as a model of feminine and wifely virtues, especially those of loyalty, faithfulness, and purity. Sītā also appears in the Vedas, where she is worshipped as a goddess presiding over vegetables and fruit, and is a personification of agriculture. Her name means 'the furrow'.

Janaka

King of Videha, in northern Bihār. This character of the Rāmāyana story has an historical existence and is mentioned in the Upanishads. He was said to have had the sage Yājnavalkya as his adviser, and to have resisted the pretensions of the Brāhmins by claiming the right to offer his own sacrifice.

Kaikeyī

A wife of Daśaratha and the mother of Bhārata. Kaikeyī nursed the king to recovery after a battle and as a reward was granted the boon of any request she cared to make. Her request was that her son should succeed the king instead of Rāma.

Rākshasas

Demons in the Rāmāyana, and the enemies of man. In addition to this mythological interpretation the Rākshasas may also have been originally a conquered non-Āryan people.

Rāvana

King of the Rākshasas and also of Śri Lanka. Rāvana was the great enemy of Rāma. In the Rāmayana the battle between Rāma and Rāvana is seen as part of the conflict between good and evil. In Vaishnavite mythology, the purpose of the incarnation of Rāma was the destruction of Rāvana.

Sugrīva

King of the monkeys, who rendered great assistance to Rāma after the abduction of Sītā.

Hanumān

The general of the monkey army, who played a major part in the destruction of the demons. Hanumān had remarkable powers, especially with regard to travel. The legends tell of him flying at great speed, and of jumping from the Indian mainland to Śri Lanka in one leap.

—

Ayodhyā

One of the sacred cities of the Hindus, and the home of Rāma, Ayodhyā is situated a few miles from Faizabad in Uttar Pradesh. It contains a great temple dedicated to Hanumān. The town also has important associations for Jains and Buddhists.

Kurukshetra

The place, to the north-west of modern Delhi, where the great battle of the Mahābhārata took place. It seems likely the story in the Epic is based upon a real battle. Widely differing suggestions are made about when such a battle may have taken place, although the probable period is within two hundred years either side of 1000 BC. According to the Mahābhārata the battle raged for eighteen days before the final victory of the Pāndavas.

Yāga

A horse-sacrifice, undertaken by king Daśaratha as a sacrifice to the gods for the gift of sons. As a result of the yāga, says the Rāmāyana, his four sons were born of his three wives. The word 'yāga' simply means 'sacrifice'.

Svayamvara

The contest at which suitors competed for the privilege of marrying a particular girl. The girl exercised her own choice of bridegroom after the contest. It was at such ceremonies that Arjuna won Draupadī for himself and his brothers and Rāma gained Sītā as his bride.

Bhagavad Gītā

Literally, 'The Song of the Lord'. The best known and most loved of Hindu scriptures, the Gītā comprises chapters twenty-five to forty-two of the Mahābhārata. The date of the composition of the Gītā is sometime between 200 BC and 200 CE. The 'Song of the Lord' is in the form of a dialogue between Arjuna and Krishna on the battlefield of Kurukshetra. Krishna appeared in the guise of Arjuna's chariot driver. Arjuna was tormented by the thought of having to engage in battle with his own kinsmen. The Gītā is Krishna's reply, which encourages Arjuna to perform his duty as a Kshatriya and fight in the battle, but within the framework of the story there is much about Indian philosophy. The Gītā emphasizes the importance of dharma related to caste duty. It contains a strong element of devotional theism. Chapter eleven of the Gītā tells of a theophany in which Krishna reveals himself in his divine form to Arjuna.

Sanjaya

The narrator of the Bhagavad Gītā. Sanjaya reports upon the events preceding the battle to the blind king Dhritarāshtra, and this device is used to set the scene of the conversation between Arjuna and Krishna.

Sāmkhya

One of the six main schools of Indian philosophy (see p. 41). Much of the teaching of the Gītā is based upon Sāmkhya.

Yoga

Another of the six schools of Indian philosophy. In the Gītā, however, the word Yoga is used to describe various means or ways which are said to lead to liberation.

Jnāna Yoga

The way of knowledge. Jnāna reflects the teaching of the Upanishads that deep reflection and introspection leading to knowledge of Brahman and his relationship to the world and the individual soul is the way that leads to liberation.

Karma Yoga

The way of action. An alternative or complement to Jnāna is the performance of right actions in the fulfilment of dharma.

Bhakti Yoga

The way of devotion. The climax of the Gītā suggests that Bhakti is not simply an alternative way to liberation, but that it is the best way of all. It portrays a loving, personal God who saves men by his grace. When all else has failed, loving devotion will suffice.

Nishkāma Karma

Actions performed without desire, and with no thought of praise or blame. The idea of disinterested action is an important part of the Gītā's teaching. It was especially emphasized by Mahatma Gāndhi when he used the Gītā as a text for his programme of non-violent resistance.

Kāma

Lust or desire which, according to the Gītā, vitiates our best actions.

5 Bhakti, or popular religion

Whilst philosophical systems contain the forms of Hinduism best known in the West, the most obvious expression of Hinduism in India is an exuberant devotional faith, expressed in dance, music, and pilgrimage, and centring upon devotion to a personal God. The word 'bhakti', or loving devotion, is the generic term for this kind of religion.

Hindus conceive the possibility of worshipping the one true God in a number of ways, by different names, and through different forms, and they see this variety as expressing the range of meaning which is in God.

Two main forms of devotional religion are found in Hinduism. In Vaishnavism the object of worship is Lord Vishnu, or one of his incarnations, such as Rāma or Krishna. In Śaivism, it is Lord Śiva or one of his consorts who is worshipped. Both Vaishnavism and Śaivism express devotion to a personal God, who saves people by his grace.

In Vaishnavism there is found the tradition of the ten avatāras, or incarnations, of Lord Vishnu, and popular devotion centres upon the seventh and eighth avatāras, Rāma and Krishna.

Bhakti encourages the development of a personal relationship with God through the use of human analogies. The human situations which parallel the relationship between God and the individual may be that of the servant's relationship with his master, the affection between two friends, the feelings between parent and child or child and parent. But the commonest analogies are the relationships between wife and husband, as in the story of Sītā and Rāma, and the beloved and her lover, as in the story of Rādhā and Krishna.

Bhakti probably has its roots deep in the prehistoric period of Indian religion. The evidence of the worship of a 'proto-Śiva' in pre-Āryan India is taken by some to be evidence for the existence of a similar kind of religion to bhakti in pre-Vedic times. Bhakti as we now know it has long been important in Dravidian South India, and in addition to lively devotional worship it has sometimes encouraged a lessening of emphasis upon caste and other traditional Hindu values.

Vaishnavism has been strongest in North India, whilst Śaivism has flourished mainly in the south, where in some forms it has developed a concept of personal sin similar to that found in Christianity.

Both Śaivism and Vaishnavism have tended to use local languages instead of, or in addition to, the sacred language of Sanskrit.

Bhakti Mārga

Mārga is a word for 'way' (and a common word for 'road' or 'street' in India). So bhakti mārga refers to those aspects of Hinduism which regard loving devotion to a personal God as the primary way of salvation.

Vishnu

One of the greatest gods of Hinduism. He appeared as a minor god in the Rig Veda (see p. 11), but Vishnu is thought to be at least partly Dravidian in origin. Certainly his importance grew considerably, so that by the time of the Epics he was one of the greatest of Hindu gods, and was regarded as the preserver of life. In the Purānas he is described as Prajāpati (creator) and Supreme God.

Vaishnavite

A worshipper of Lord Vishnu. In devotional religion Hindus are usually either Vaishnavite or Śaivite (worshippers of Śiva). A mark of identification sometimes worn by the Vaishnavite is a grouping of three vertical lines on the forehead, forming a trident design.

Vaishnavism

That part of Hinduism devoted to the worship of Vishnu or one of his avatāras or consorts, such as Rāma, Krishna, or Lakshmi. The origins of Vaishnavism are obscure, but it is likely that it was a non-Āryan element which grew in importance between the rise of Buddhism and the beginning of the Christian era. The emphasis of Vaishnavism is upon devotional worship. It has sometimes been anti-Brāhmin in its attitudes.

Śeśa

In Vaishnavite mythology Śeśa is a thousand-headed serpent who formed a bed on the floor of the ocean for Vishnu to sleep on before the creation of the world.

Vaikuntha

The highest heaven, in which Lord Vishnu reigns. This is sometimes said to be located on Mount Meru.

Garuda

A mythical creature who is said to provide a mount for Vishnu. Garuda is depicted as having the body and limbs of a man and the head and talons of an eagle.

Lakshmī

The goddess of good fortune and prosperity, and a consort of Vishnu. The word Lakshmī is used in the Rig Veda with the meaning of 'good fortune'. A legend of the Rāmāyana describes Lakshmī emerging from the ocean as a fully-formed female beauty, holding a lotus in her hand. Lakshmī is said to have been associated with the avatāras of Lord Vishnu in a series of reincarnations, as Padmā and Dharanī and Rukminī and Sītā.

Avatāra

Literally, 'one who descends'. In Vaishnavism there developed the tradition that Lord Vishnu was reborn repeatedly in order to meet particular needs. The main Vaishnavite tradition maintains that there are ten avatāras, of whom nine have already appeared. But there are alternative traditions. The Bhagavata Purāna lists twenty-two avatāras, and a school of Bengali Vaishnavism offers a theory of twenty-four avatāras, thus making room for some more modern and historical figures.

Ishtadeva

Ishta means 'desired' or 'sought after', and Ishtadeva means the desired god, in the sense of a manifestation of God chosen by the worshipper as the one most conducive to his or her spiritual development. For Vaishnavites, Vishnu or one of his avatāras or consorts would be an Ishtadeva.

The Ten Avatāras of Lord Vishnu

Matsya

The fish. According to the legend Vishnu took this form in order to save a sage, Vaivaswata or Manu, from a great flood. The Bhagavata Purāna adds to the story of the flood an incident in which a demon carried off the Veda which had come from the mouth of the sleeping Brahmā. Matsya instructed Manu and the Rishis in the doctrines of the Veda, then slew the demon and restored the Veda to Brahmā.

Kūrma

During another flood objects indispensable to the continuing work of creation were lost. Vishnu descended in the form of Kūrma, a tortoise, and lent his back for a pivot on which Mount Mandara could be turned as a stick for churning the ocean. In the churning of the seas the lost objects were recovered.

Varāha

The boar whose form Vishnu took in order to raise up the earth from the bottom of the sea, to which it had been consigned by a demon. Originally a legend of Brahmā, the story was applied later to Vishnu.

Narasimha

A man-lion. This legend tells of a demon-king who had been given great powers by Brahmā and had become invulnerable to any harm from gods, men, or animals. Brahmā had promised that the king (Hiranyakaśipu) could not be killed by day or night, inside or outside the house. When the wicked king's actions became intolerable Vishnu took the form of a man-lion (neither man nor beast) and killed the king at the entrance to his house (neither inside nor outside) at dusk (neither day nor night). So in spite of all its powers, the demon was destroyed by Vishnu.

Vāmana

The story of Vāmana also concerns a king, Bali, who had become too powerful. Bali was a good king, but his ambition seemed to threaten even the territory of the gods. In their alarm the gods caused Vishnu to be born as Vāmana, who grew up as a dwarf. Vāmana then approached king Bali and asked for a gift of three paces of land. In view of the diminutive stature of Vāmana, Bali readily agreed. But then Vāmana grew to enormous size and covered the whole world in two strides. The area which would have been covered by the third stride, the infernal regions, were left to Bali.

Paraśurāma

Literally this means 'Rāma-with-the-axe', and was a form taken by Vishnu at a time when the Kshatriya class were tyrannizing all men and usurping the power of the Brāhmins. The historical analogies of the legend are thus fairly clear. The stories of Paraśurāma include that of a Kshatriya king who visited the hermitage home of Paraśurāma's family and stole their wonderful cow, Kāmadhenu, who supplied every good thing that men desired. Paraśurāma pursued the king, slew him with his axe, and restored the cow to its rightful home.

Rāma

The seventh avatāra, and the hero of the Rāmāyana (see p. 19). The purpose of Vishnu's incarnation as Rāma is seen to be the defeat of evil, personified by Rāvana and the Rākshasas, and the establishment of a kingdom of righteousness and peace. It should be noted that the battle was also in some sense a north-south conflict in India.

Krishna

The eighth avatāra, celebrated in the stories of the Mahābhārata and the Purānas. With Rāma and Krishna the list of avatāras begins to include figures with possible historical antecedents.

The purpose of the birth and life of Krishna according to the legend was to defeat an evil king who had come to power. When king Kamsa heard of the birth of Krishna he sought to destroy all the young children in the place. The baby Krishna was taken to Vrindāvana to be brought up by Nanda and Yaśodā, a simple family of cowherds of the Yādava tribe. It was here when he grew up that Krishna had his amorous adventures with the local girls, whose desire for him is seen as an analogy of the human desire for God. Krishna did eventually achieve the aim of killing king Kamsa, although this by no means ended his adventures. The events of the Mahābhārata are placed after Krishna's revenge on the king.

Buddha

An unexpected name in this list, and there are two possible explanations for the inclusion of Buddha here. The first is that his name may have been included in order to incorporate Buddhism into the Hindu system by appropriating the success of Buddhism to the

Brāhmin cause. The second is that the intention may have been to discredit Buddha by portraying him as the avatāra who comes at the end of the age to mislead men and hasten the decline of religion.

Kalki

The avatāra who is still to come. It is said that Kalki will come riding on a white horse and with sword in hand. He will destroy the wicked, and bring this present age to an end.

Bhagavān

A title, meaning 'worshipful' or 'Lord', which is frequently used of Lord Vishnu.

Bhāgavatas

Worshippers of Vishnu and Krishna. The rise of the sect of Bhāgavatas in the last century CE marks the beginning of Vaishnavism. At first the Bhāgavatas worshipped Vasudeva, who came to be identified with Krishna and Vishnu.

Purānas

Texts of devotional, and especially Vaishnavite, religion. In all there are eighteen main Purānas, ranging in dates of writing from the sixth to the sixteenth century CE but containing material from a much older period. They provide a stimulus for an extreme form of bhakti, and contain many stories of miracles. Purāna means 'olden times'. The Purānas are part of smriti, but are regarded by Vaishnavites as very important scriptures.

Bhāgavata Purāna

The most celebrated of the Purānas. The date of this work is uncertain, but it probably dates from the thirteenth century CE. The tenth book of the Bhāgavata Purāna contains the story of Krishna. The story is in the form of a dialogue between a sage and a king. The king has been condemned to death for killing a holy man. In order to stimulate his devotion and so ensure his salvation he spends the week before his death listening to the stories of Krishna. The text contains much about the love between Krishna and the gopīs.

Vāsudeva

Actually the name of Krishna's father, according to the Mahābhārata. But the name was also applied to Krishna, and is then said to derive from the word for 'the indweller', referring to the idea of Krishna dwelling in all beings.

Devaki

The wife of Vāsudeva and mother of Krishna.

Kamsa

King at the time of Krishna's birth, and a cousin of Devakī. There was a prophecy that Kamsa would be killed by Devakī's eighth son, and so Kamsa attempted to kill all her children. The infant Krishna was taken away secretly to Gokula. The parallels between the stories of Krishna and those of Moses and Jesus have often been drawn. After Krishna had grown up he killed king Kamsa and seized the kingdom of Mathurā.

Nanda
Yaśodā

Nanda was a cowherd, and Yaśodā his wife. The couple looked after Krishna during his early years when he was in hiding from king Kamsa.

Vrindāvana

The forest of Vrindā, in the district of Mathurā, where Krishna lived in exile under the assumed name of Gopāla. The name Vrindā is also an alternative name for Rādhā.

Gopis

The cowgirls or shepherdesses who fell passionately in love with Krishna. When Krishna played his flute, the story says, the gopīs could not help but leave their homes or their husbands and go to meet him.

Rādhā

The favourite love of Krishna. Vaishnavite literature contains vivid stories, many of them in erotic form, about the love of Rādhā and Krishna. Their love is regarded as an analogy of divine-human love. Rādhā was the wife of a cowherd named Ayanaghosha, but left her husband to become Krishna's mistress.

The stories of Rādhā and Krishna are fairly late, being found in Vaishnavite literature from the tenth century CE. Rādhā occupied an important position in the Vaishnavism of Bengal, but in southern India there was less enthusiasm for the eroticism of the stories about her. Rādhā was considered by some to be an incarnation of Lakshmī.

Rukminī

The daughter of Bhīshmaka and another consort of Krishna. Krishna married Rukmiṇī, and she became his principal wife, bearing him ten sons and a daughter.

Pradyumna

The eldest son of Krishna and Rukmiṇī. According to one legend, Pradyumna was a reincarnation of Kāma, the god of love.

Balarāma

The elder brother of Krishna. Balarāma had a very fair complexion, in contrast with the dark-skinned Krishna. He and Krishna grew up together, and shared many adventures.

Dvārakā

The new capital of Krishna after the defeat of Kamsa. The city, in Gujarāt, was said to have been submerged under the sea seven days after the death of Krishna.

Yādavas

The community to which Krishna belonged. The Yādavas are thought to have been of low caste (and possibly non-Āryan) origin.

Māyon

A name given to the pastoral Krishna in early Tamil anthologies, which contain the first references to Krishna. Māyon is a Tamil word for 'black'.

Yuga

In Hindu cosmology the Yugas are four immensely long periods of time by which the cycle of the world's life is divided. The four are the Kṛita Yuga, the Treta Yuga, the Dvāpara Yuga, and the Kāli Yuga.

Kāli Yuga

The present age, with a duration of 432,000 years.

Ālvārs

Twelve great poet-saints of Tamil Vaishnavism who lived between the seventh and tenth centuries CE. Their poetry expresses strong devotion, directed towards Lord Krishna. The poems were collected together during the tenth century under the title Nālāyiram. They stress a salvation by grace which is open to all, regardless of caste. The vigorous devotional movement of the Ālvārs fostered the development of Tamil bhakti and the spread of Vaishnavism. A synthesis between this devotional religion and more orthodox Hinduism culminated in the work of Rāmānuja.

Nimbārka

A South Indian philosopher, he taught that Krishna is the Supreme Being towards whom devotion should be cultivated. In the last resort, however, it is Krishna's grace which makes possible the vision of God. Nimbārka was the founder of the Sānaka school of Vaishnavism. His dates are uncertain, but he probably lived in the early fourteenth century CE.

Madhva

A Vaishnavite philosopher of the early thirteenth century who was concerned to refute Advaita doctrine. Madhva developed a doctrine of dualism, or dvaita, and is associated with the Brahma school of Vaishnavism (see p. 45).

Vallabha

A Telegu Brāhmin of the late fifteenth and early sixteenth centuries who was associated with the Rudra school. His teaching laid strong emphasis upon bhakti and upon the cult of Rādhā and Krishna.

The Four Main Schools of Vaishnavism

Śrī

The word means 'fortune' or 'prosperity', and is one of the titles given to Lakshmī, a consort of Vishnu. It is also used of one of the sects of Vaishnavism associated with the great teacher Rāmānuja, the founder of the Visishtadvaita school (see pp. 44f.). In the Śrī Sampradāya (or sect) Brahman is regarded as having two aspects, personal and impersonal.

Vadakalai

Later followers of Rāmānuja developed his ideas, and among them there arose two notions of salvation and grace. According to the northern school, or Vadakalai, salvation was analogous to the experience of the baby monkey carried by his mother: the young monkey has to hold on to his mother by his own efforts. So, said the Vadakalai school, although salvation is through God's grace it does require the co-operation of man.

Thenkalai

The other group among Rāmānuja's followers constituted the southern school, or Thenkalai. They regarded salvation as being analogous to the kitten which is picked up by the scruff of its neck and carried by its mother. No effort is required. So, they said, salvation is through grace alone.

Sānaka

The school of Vaishnavite philosophy founded by Nimbārka. A form of bhedābheda (difference – non-difference). Sānaka held that souls remain distinct from God even though they are offshoots of him. Sānaka also taught that Rādhā and Krishna embody the supreme will and the supreme love.

—

Brahma

The Vaishnavite sect associated with Madhva, in which God and man are regarded as quite distinct from each other.

Rudra

In which souls are regarded as being different in their nature from each other because of the desire of God for play, or lila, in his creation. The individual must cultivate a hunger for God like that of the shepherdesses for Krishna. This sect was originally led by Vallabha.

Rāmānanda

A fourteenth-century Vaishnavite, and a member of the school of Rāmānuja. In most respects his teaching was similar to that of Rāmānuja. He used the name of Rāma for God, and advocated fervent devotional worship. He opposed caste distinctions, and admitted people to his sect regardless of caste background. His ideas were influential in later times among those who attempted to find common ground between Hindus and Muslims.

Chaitanya

A Bengali who founded an important Vaishnavite sect. Chaitanya lived from 1485 until 1534. He regarded Krishna as the supreme God and all other deities as manifestations of him. His emotional bhakti religion attracted many followers, including women and low-caste people, and he has been a continuing influence among bhaktis. He also emphasized the value of Nām Jappa, or chanting the sacred name of Krishna.

Tulsi Dās

A poet who lived in the sixteenth and seventeenth centuries, and was in the tradition of Rāmānanda. His main work was the popular Hindi version of the Rāmāyana, which differs in many significant

respects from the original, but which strongly reinforces the bhakti
tradition in which Tulsi Dās stood.

Śiva

One of the three great gods of Hinduism, Śiva evolved from the
Rudra of the Rig Veda. He is regarded as the god of creation and
destruction. In his role as the destroyer he is thought of as being
found in such places as cremation grounds and battlefields. Sometimes he is depicted wearing a garland of skulls. But Śiva is also the
great ascetic, and patron of the Yogis. In this role Śiva is said to sit on
Mount Kailāsa, in the Himālayas, and maintain the world through
his meditation.

Natarājan

Śiva in his role as 'Lord of the Dance', the cosmic dance of destruction and recreation. The image of the 'Lord of the Dance', or
Natarājan, is very popular in India, and especially so in the Tamil
country, where religious dance has long been part of tradition.

Śaivism

That sect of Hinduism devoted to the worship of Śiva. It is probable
that Śaivism has roots in pre-Āryan religion (see p. 5). Śaivism does
not subscribe to the idea of avatāras, but is strongly monotheistic.
A mark of identification sometimes worn by the Śaivite is composed
of two or three horizontal lines, with a dot below or in the centre,
made on the forehead with white or grey ash.

The literature of Śaivism is almost exclusively Sanskrit or Tamil.

Pārvatī

A name of the wife of Śiva, Pārvatī means 'the mountaineer'. She is
also known simply as Devī, 'goddess'. She is said to be the daughter
of Himavat, or the Himālayan mountains. She is the Śakti, or female
energy, of Śiva, and as such has both a beneficent and a terrible
aspect.

Durgā

'The inaccessible': Śiva's wife in her terrible form. It is possible that
Durgā, who according to the Mahābhārata was fond of meat and
wine, was a pre-Āryan deity.

Kālī

'The black one', another manifestation of Devī in her terrible and
destructive aspect. Kālī is portrayed with a hideous face, long fangs,
a great tongue dripping with blood, and wearing a necklace of skulls.

It was in her honour that the Thuggees, or Thugs, committed their murders.

Nandi

A humped-back bull, milky-white in colour, who is the traditional mount of Śiva.

Paśupati

Śiva as Lord of the beasts, and in this form regarded as the patron of reproduction in men, beasts and plants, and also worshipped in the form of the linga.

Śaiva Siddhānta

An important school of Śaivism in South India from the seventh century CE onwards. This school has made a notable contribution to devotional religion, and has produced a profound philosophy. The texts of Śaiva Siddhānta are in Tamil, and include contributions from members of various caste groups.

Śaiva Siddhānta teaches that worship demands both subject and object, that salvation comes from reliance upon Śiva as saviour and the acceptance of discipline under a guru who reflects Śiva's nature. Śaiva Siddhānta combines monotheism, a deep sense of sin, and concepts of great divine and human love. The last great classical writing of Śaiva Siddhānta, and one of its basic texts, is the Śiva-Jnāna-Bodham of the thirteenth century.

Pati

The Lord as personal creator in Śaiva Siddhānta. The word is said to stand for Paśupati as 'Lord of souls'.

Paśu

The souls of men, which are of the same essence as Śiva but are not identical with him.

Pāśa

Bond, or matter. In Śaivite philosophy, Pāśa is that by which the perception of the soul is limited.

Shakti

Energy, will, or power, and so the manifestation of Śiva in these forms.

Anbu

The Tamil word for 'love, attachment, or friendship'. The idea of love between God and man is important in Śaiva Siddhānta.

Arul

The Tamil word for 'grace'. It is by grace that the soul is finally enlightened by Śiva.

6 Hindu philosophy

Religion in India has always had close connections with philosophy, and philosophy has usually been regarded as a genuinely religious activity. The period of the Upanishads was a time of intense philosophical reflection, producing literature of great profundity and insight. It has been seen how the early practical religion of the Rig Veda gave way to the reflexive thought of the Upanishads and to an attitude to the great questions of life and death which are now regarded as typically Hindu.

The questions, about reincarnation and karma, about the nature of reality and our perception of the phenomenal world, about the existence of a personal God or an impersonal Absolute, continued to be discussed throughout the centuries between the writing of the Upanishads and 'the Christian era. Those centuries saw, of course, the rise of Buddhism and its challenge to Hindu thought and practice, and the development of the bhakti cults which circumvented many of the philosophical issues and concentrated instead upon direct spiritual experience.

Gradually there developed a number of different philosophical schools. The development had begun by the time the Upanishads were completed, but it continued for many centuries. Indeed, a great time for the philosophical schools in Hinduism came during what in Europe was known as the medieval period. Between 800 and 1300 CE there was much philosophical activity in India. Ideas came to be more clearly defined, much dispute and argument took place, and scholars and others committed themselves to particular schools of thought. This was the period in which some of the most important of the philosophical schools of Hinduism arose, although the ideas which they propounded were often reformulations of earlier teaching.

The middle period, between 800 and 1300 CE, was a time when

other factors besides pure philosophical enquiry were at work. It was a time of mixing of ideas between the Āryan north and the Dravidian south of India. Some of the greatest philosophers were southerners who as well as imbibing their own Dravidian language and culture studied the Sanskrit scriptures and travelled extensively in other parts of India. This cross-fertilization bore fruit in some of the philosophical schools.

During the earlier part of the middle period Buddhism was also a great power in the land. One Hindu answer to Buddhism had been expressed in the bhakti cults. Now some Hindu philosophers, like Śankara, tried to meet Buddhism on its own ground by producing Hindu philosophy which could provide systems as subtle and comprehensive as the Buddhist.

Of the six main schools of Hindu philosophy, three are of only minor importance. But the other three, Sāmkhya, Yoga, and Vedānta, have continued to be of enormous importance in India and beyond, and a knowledge of these three systems is indispensable to an understanding of Hinduism.

Hindu philosophy covers a wide spectrum. Some of it is atheistic, some is monistic, some is theistic. In the period between 1000 and 1300 CE one crucial issue was the nature of Brahman, or God. Should Brahman be thought of as Ultimate Reality, or the Absolute, an impersonal force permeating all life and providing the clue to a proper understanding of existence, yet not amenable to worship and devotion? Or could one speak of a God with personal qualities, who loves those who worship him and offers them his grace for their salvation?

Within the broad spectrum of Vedānta different schools arose to provide different answers to these questions. In the eighth and ninth centuries CE Śankara propounded a doctrine of strict monism, or Advaita, in which Brahman was regarded as the impersonal Absolute, and a personal God was seen as at best a concession to the less enlightened who may need the crutch of worship in order to climb to the heights of Advaita.

It was partly in reaction against the teaching of Śankara that Rāmānuja produced his philosophy of Visishtadvaita, which claimed to be true to the best insights of Advaita whilst avoiding its worst faults. Visishtadavaita gave an important place to a personal God, and so provided a philosophy which could coalesce with and support bhakti.

The philosophical tradition of Hinduism has continued to be rich and varied. Until recent times many Western observers of Hinduism have concluded too readily that the Advaita of Śankara was the definitive philosophical position for all Hindus. This was not so in

the past, and it is not so today. There remain alternative interpretations, of which Advaita is but one.

The six schools of Indian philosophy

Nyāya

The name means 'rule', 'standard' or 'right', and the Nyāya is
concerned with logical argument and proof. It regards ignorance as
the root of suffering and transmigration, and teaches that liberation
should be obtained through knowledge. The original teacher of this
system, whose dates are unknown but who lived some time between
the beginnings of the Buddhist and Christian eras, was Akshapāda
Gautama.

Nyāya was originally secular in outlook, although it later developed
theistic elements. The later Nyāya schools formulated the idea of
four pramāna, or 'means of knowledge'. These are: Pratyaksa, or
perception; Anumāna, or inference; Upamāna, or inference by
analogy or comparison; Sabda, or 'word', which meant reference to
written authorities such as the Vedas. The text of this school, the
Nyāya Sutra, written sometime between the second century BC and
the second century CE, is also a basic text for Indian logic.

Vaiśeshika

Vaiśeshika, or individualism, is an atomistic theory of the universe. It
teaches that there are millions of souls, all different in condition as a
result of karma. Each element has its own individual characteristics,
or viśeśas. But there is a clear distinction drawn between these
individual atoms and the substances of space, time, soul, and mind,
which are known as dravyas. Vaiśeshika, therefore, teaches a dualism
of souls and matter.

This system was originally more of an early scientific approach
than a religious one, but in the course of time it coalesced with
Nyāya and there began the development of some metaphysics. In its
composite form Nyāya-Vaiśeshika pondered the question of whether
the external world has a real and enduring existence outside the
minds which observe it. The conclusion that the external world does
have an independent existence made the system a form a Realism.
In contrast with some other schools, Nyāya-Vaiśeshika taught that
Ultimate Reality is many, not one.

Mīmāmsā (Pūrva Mīmāmsā)

Mīmāmsā refers to a discussion or exegesis of a sacred text, whilst
'Pūrva Mīmāmsā' simply means 'earlier exegesis'. In the Mīmāmsā
the point of exploring the texts of the Vedas was to ensure the correct

performance of ritual and sacrifice. The system emphasizes ritual rather than philosophy. There is little attention given to belief, for it is correct action rather than knowledge which is thought to convey benefit. The Nyāya, Vaiśeshika, and Mīmāmsā are all of minor importance. The three schools which follow have been by far the most influential forms of Indian philosophy.

Sāmkhya

The word means 'reflection' or 'enumeration'. Sāmkhya arose perhaps a little before Buddhism, with which it shares a number of important ideas. It has a meagre literature, but a basic early text is the Sāmkhya Kārikā of Īshvara Krishna, written between the seventh and fifth centuries BC. There is a reaction in Sāmkhya against the monism of the Upanishads.

According to Sāmkhya philosophy, the universe contains two independent entities, which it calls Purusha and Prakriti. Prakriti corresponds to the phenomenal world, and Purusha to the spiritual reality which is said to give meaning and direction to the flux of material life. The complexity of Prakriti is caused by the existence and combination of three qualities, or gunas. The three are: sattva, or virtue, which stands for whatever is fine and pure; rajas, or passion, which stands for whatever is active and vigorous; tamas, or dullness. The three gunas are said to be present in all people, and the predominant guna determines the personality type. Because of the conflicting action of the three gunas, Prakriti is said to be a combination of happiness, misery and delusion. One of the basic problems of man, according to Sāmkhya, is that māyā operates within the world to persuade people that Prakriti is the whole of reality. Yet it is ignorance which causes man to overlook the existence of Purusha, or to fail to see through the ever-present Prakriti to the spiritual values of Purusha which alone give meaning and direction to Prakriti. When a person acquires true knowledge, then he is able to discern Purusha free from the shackles of Prakriti.

One of the great goals of life, according to the Sāmkhya Kārikā, is to put an end to 'the three kinds of suffering', which are diseases of the body, pain caused by men or beasts, or pain caused by the elements. Suffering is caused by wrong knowledge, which identifies Purusha with Prakriti. For misery is to be found only in Prakriti, and not in Purusha. Sāmkhya rejected the idea of a personal god. It influenced the development of the Jaina and Buddhist religions and its teaching underlies a large part of the Bhagavad Gītā.

Yoga

Yoga is a school of philosophy rather than just a set of exercises.

Yoga means 'to join together', although the system of spiritual, mental, and physical exercises which developed under the name of Yoga emphasized liberation, or isolation, rather more than it did union with God. Yoga shares some of the assumptions of Sāmkhya, and from them derives the idea that the important thing in the religious life is to secure the liberation of Purusha from Prakriti. Yoga conceives of the mind as having three basic components: manas, the recording faculty; buddhi, or discrimination; ahamkāra, the sense of 'I'. Yoga sets out a system of disciplined development which aims at bringing mind, body and spirit under control. The physical postures and exercises which are the most familiar part of Yoga are intended to secure control of the body and the mind as necessary preliminaries to spiritual control. Patanjali defined Yoga as 'the control of the functioning of the mind'. The qualities necessary for the practice of Yoga are said to include high intelligence, good memory, and faith (faith in the efficacy of the process).

Unlike Sāmkhya, Yoga does have a place for a personal God. Indeed, a verse of the Yoga Sūtra suggests 'devotion to God' as an alternative method of achieving what otherwise is to be gained by strenuous effort.

The basic text of Yoga is the Yoga Sūtra of Patanjali, written between 300 and 500 CE. It provides detailed guidance on the practice of Yoga, and describes eight limbs, or steps, which are all necessary to the successful pursuit of Yoga:

(i) **Yama** A series of moral obligations, consisting of non-violence, truthfulness, chastity, and refraining from stealing and covetousness. Yama means 'self-restraint'.

(ii) **Niyama** 'Limitation' or 'restraint'. Niyama is concerned with ritual purity, especially in matters of eating and drinking, purity of thought, happiness or contentment with one's lot, and self-denial.

(iii) **Āsana** The postures and exercises which aim at the control of the body in order that physical preoccupations should not be a barrier to spiritual progress.

(iv) **Prānāyāma** Breath-control, often practised in conjunction with the physical postures and also intended to bring complete physical control.

(v) **Pratyāhārana** 'Withdrawal'. At this stage the yogi is expected to withdraw his mind from the preoccupations and distractions of everyday life.

(vi) **Dhārana** Concentrating the mind on one particular object, which may be a picture, a religious ornament, a verse of scripture, or any other suitable object.

(vii) **Dhyāna** Contemplation, in which one's own thoughts deepen and extend on the object of concentration. At this stage the yogi should be able to receive ideas and impressions which come to him.

(viii) **Samādhi**   Trance, or mystical awareness, in which a person should not be conscious of himself, but only of the object of contemplation.

Hatha Yoga

The physical aspect of Yoga, especially the postures, exercises, and breathing.

Rāja Yoga

The whole system of discipline, concerned with mental and spiritual attainment as well as physical control.

Advaita Vedānta

Advaita means 'non-dual', and Advaita Vedānta is the school of Indian philosophy best known in the West. Its teaching is based upon the Upanishads, and particularly those texts which teach a monistic doctrine. Parallels between Advaita and such Western philosophers as Hegel, Schelling, and F. H. Bradley can readily be drawn. Advaita teaches that our knowledge of the phenomenal world is full of contradictions, and that only the Absolute, or Brahman, is wholly real. The world experienced through the senses is little more than a dream. It is because of the operation of māyā that the world appears to be full of different and contradictory objects. If we could see things as they are we should recognize that there is only one reality and that there is no difference between the individual soul and Brahman. Modern exponents of Advaita include Swami Vivekananda and Dr S. Radhakrishnan. They have presented Advaita to the West as the highest form of Indian philosophy.

—

Gaudapāda

The first important exponent of Advaita, Gaudapāda wrote a commentary on the Māndūkya Upanishad, which is one of the basic texts of the school. Gaudapāda was a thoroughgoing monist who regarded the phenomenal world as a gigantic illusion, purely subjective in its nature. He taught that only Brahman truly exists, and denied the possibility of change and the validity of causation.

Śankara

A South Indian Brāhmin who lived in the eighth and ninth centuries CE, probably from 788 until 820. Like Gaudapāda, Śankara believed that the impressions of the phenomenal world which we receive delude

us as to the true nature of reality. In this, he agreed, the action of māyā
plays an important part. But for Śankara the world is not a complete
illusion. He believed that there is something real experienced through
our senses, even though we are misled as to its true nature. Our
experience of the world he compared to a dream. There is a sense in
which a dream is real, and a sense in which it is an illusion. Nevertheless, only the Absolute, or Brahman, is totally real. Śankara was a
great teacher and dialectician, and his teaching was very successful.
His interpretation of Indian philosophy is still the best known outside India.

Visishtadvaita

A school of limited non-dualism which evolved in South India out of
criticism of Śankara's teaching and an original contribution to Indian
philosophy made by Rāmānuja. Among objections to Advaita were
the questions of how, if Brahman is all that truly exists, this world of
illusion came into being in the first place; and of what could Brahman
be conscious if he is properly described as perfect consciousness?
There was also dissatisfaction with Advaita because it was so intellectual a scheme, and gave only limited recognition to devotional
religion and a personal God. Visishtadvaita means 'non-dualism with
distinctions'. The philosophy began with the teaching of Rāmānuja,
who taught that the phenomenal world is real and the māyā is God's
mode of operation in the world. In Visishtadvaita God is not simply
the impersonal Brahman, but a personal being who expresses his love
through relationships. Indidivual souls and the phenomenal world
are the 'body' of Brahman, and Brahman, or God, is in the world as
the soul is in the body. The individual soul retains its self-cons-
ciousness even if it attains to communion with God. The Ātman, or
self, whilst essentially pure consciousness and the same substance as
God, is not to be identified with God. Likewise the liberated soul is
one with God, and yet still distinct from him.

Visishtadvaita is an important philosophy, especially in South
India. It succeeded in reconciling the teaching of the Upanishads
with devotional religion.

Rāmānuja

An eleventh-century Tamil Brāhmin (his dates are sometimes given
as 1017 to 1137, although his birth is likely to have been later than
this suggests), and the founder of the Visishtadvaita school. Rāmānuja
was born in Tamilnādu, near Madras, and wandered all over India
before settling at Śrirangam. He wrote commentaries on the Vedānta,
the Brahma Sūtra, and the Bhagavadgītā. His commentary on the
Vedānta Sūtra, the Śribhāshya, is a classical text for Vaishnavites.

Rāmānuja saw the world as an expression of God's need to be loved. Brahman, he argued, is not simply an impersonal Absolute but a loving God who seeks a response from his creatures.

Rāmānuja was not only a great philosopher, for he is still revered as one of the.foremost Vaishnavite saints. He did much to relate philosophy to living religious experience.

Dvaita

The word means 'dual', and refers to a school founded in the thirteenth century as part of the Vaishnavite movement. Dvaita taught that God, souls, and matter are eternally distinct. It distinguished three classes of souls: a few elect souls who are destined for communion with God; the majority, who are bound to an endless cycle of rebirths; the depraved, who will receive punishment in hell. According to Dvaita, God saves people by his grace. Good works and even devotion do not avail without the prior action of grace.

Dvaita is an extreme expression of Vaishnavism, and it has often been suggested that the movement was influenced by Christian theology. The Syrian Church of Kerala, a neighbouring state to the one in which Dvaita developed, has existed in India since at least the fourth century and perhaps even earlier.

Madhva

A thirteenth-century Kanarese philosopher, and founder of the Dvaita school. He was born in 1197 near Mangalore, on the West coast of India, and died about 1280. Madhva was strongly opposed to Advaita philosophy because of its incompatibility with Vaishnavite devotionalism. There are many parallels between the stories of his life and the life of Christ. There are stories of him teaching learned men in the temple at an early age, walking on the water, stilling a storm at sea, and multiplying loaves and fishes. Madhva influenced Vaishnavite bhakti, but was too far removed from the main stream of Hindu thought to have any lasting significance.

Vāyu (Vaiyu)

The breath or wind, and one of the gods of the Rig Veda (see p. 10). Madhva was regarded by some of his followers as an incarnation of Vāyu, and so regarded as the 'spirit', an intermediary between God and man. There are possible parallels between this notion and the Christian doctrine of the Holy Spirit.

Bibliography

R. D. Baird and A. Bloom, *Indian and Far Eastern Religions*, Harper & Row, New York 1971

A. L. Basham, *The Wonder that was India* (1954), 3rd revised ed., Sidgwick & Jackson 1967, Taplinger, New York 1968

S. G. F. Brandon (ed.), *A Dictionary of Comparative Religion*, Weidenfeld & Nicolson and Scribner's, New York 1970

Swami Chidbhavananda, *The Bhagavad Gita*, Tapovanam Publishing House, Tirupparaitturai 1965

V. G. Childe, *New Light on the Most Ancient East* (1934), 4th ed., Routledge & Kegan Paul 1952, Praeger, New York 1953

W. T. de Bary (ed.), *Sources of Indian Tradition*, Columbia University Press 1958, reissued in 2 vols. 1964

M. Dhavamony, *Love of God according to Saiva Siddhānta*, Oxford University Press 1971

J. Dowson, *A Classical Dictionary of Hindu Mythology* (1878), 10th ed., Routledge & Kegan Paul 1968

S. P. Gupta and K. S. Ramachandran (eds.), *Mahabharata, Myth and Reality*, Agam Prakashan, Delhi 1976

M. Hiriyanna, *The Essentials of Indian Philosophy*, Allen & Unwin and Macmillan, New York 1959

Veronica Ions, *Indian Mythology*, Hamlyn 1967

E. J. Lott, *God and the Universe in theVedantic Theology of Ramanuja*, Ramanuja Research Society, Madras 1977

R. C. Majumdar, H. C. Raychaudhuri and K. Datta, *An Advanced History of India*, 2nd ed., Macmillan 1950

Juan Mascaro (trs.), *The Bhagavad Gita*, Penguin 1962

K. S. Murty, *Revelation and Reason in Advaita Vedanta*, Andhra University 1959

Swami Prabhavananda, *The Spiritual Heritage of India*, Allen & Unwin 1962, Doubleday, New York 1963

S. Radhakrishnan and C. A. Moore (eds.), *A Sourcebook in Indian Philosophy*, Princeton and Oxford University Presses 1957

C. Rajagopalachari (trs.), *Ramayana*, 3rd ed., Bhaitya Vidya Bhavan, Bombay 1958

J. M. Sarval, *The Bhagavata Purana*, Calcutta 1930–34

N. Smart, *Hindu Patterns of Liberation*, Open University 1978

K. C. Varachari, *Viśishtādvaita and its Development*, Chakravarthy Publications, Tirupati 1969

B. Walker, *The Hindu World*, Allen & Unwin and Praeger, 1968

R. E. M. Wheeler, *The Indus Civilization*, Cambridge U.P. 1953

J. H. Woods, *The Yoga System of Patanjali*, Harvard Oriental Series, Motilal Banarsidas, Delhi 1966

R. C. Zaehner, *Hinduism*, Oxford University Press 1966

7 Jainism

Jainism was an early reform movement in India which developed into a separate religion. It took its form as an organized religion under Mahāvīra (sixth century BC), who was once regarded by Western scholars as the founder of Jainism, but that title is now accorded to Pārśva, who lived about 250 years earlier. Mahāvīra appears to have adapted the teaching of Pārśva and established the disciplined order of monks which has always been an important part of Jainism. The whole movement, from Pārśva onwards, was part of the questioning of Brāhmanical practice which led to departures from earlier tradition, of which the most notable were the Jaina and Buddhist movements.

Jainism was a rival of early Buddhism and there is some evidence that the Jainas, like the Buddhists, encountered opposition and persecution from Hindus.

Jaina religion has always laid great stress on asceticism, which has been carried to excess by some of its followers (Mahāvīra, for example, is said to have died from self-starvation). The word 'Jaina' is derived from the root 'ji', which means 'to conquer', and relates to the idea of the conquest of the body by the spirit. There is considerable emphasis upon karma and the need for a vigorous asceticism, including a rigorous application of non-violence, in order to avoid accumulating bad karma. This had the effect of making the monk the serious practitioner of Jainism, whilst the layman can only support the monk, obey the rules prescribed for the laity, and so gradually improve his spiritual status through the long cycle of rebirths. The importance given to non-violence may have been in part a reaction against the Brāhmin practice of animal sacrifice. The whole ascetical emphasis of Jainism influenced the Hindu tradition and contributed to the life-renouncing element in Indian religion which is so significant and yet so different from the earlier Āryan religion.

Historical developments in Jainism led to the formation of many sects, the best known of which are treated below. But the differences were always matters of emphasis rather than of fundamental beliefs.

Jainism did not maintain a numerically strong following. In its earlier years it had the support of a number of kings, and so had its periods of power, but it declined numerically with the rise of the bhakti cults. Today there are about two million Jainas in India. But the religion has continued to influence Hinduism strongly, particularly in its ascetic approach to life, the encouraging of fasting, and the practice of non-violence. The Jaina doctrine of ahimsā has been especially important in this century because it exerted considerable influence upon Mahatma Gāndhi when he formulated his policy of non-violent resistance as part of the Independence Movement in India.

Philosophically, Jainism has some similarities with Sāmkhya. Its chief centres of influence are in Gujarāt and Mysore.

Jaina (Jain)

The word is derived from the root 'ji', 'to conquer'. The Jaina is one who has conquered the body and the material world.

Pārśva (Pārśvanātha)

Thought to be the founder of the movement that became known as 'Jainism', Pārśva was born in Varanasi c. 850 BC, and was the son of a local Rājah, king Aśvasena. Little is known about his life. It is thought that his teaching included four of the five vows (or vratas) which became binding upon monks. These were: non-violence, including a regard for all living things; truthfulness; not stealing; and not coveting. Pārśva is now regarded by Jainas as the twenty-third of the twenty-four Tīrthankaras.

Mahāvīra

Once thought to have been the founder of Jainism, Mahāvīra is now regarded as a reformer and propagator of the teaching of Pārśva. He lived in the sixth century BC. Orthodox Jaina tradition accepts the dates of 599 – 527 BC for his life, although most modern authorities date his death around 468 and his birth correspondingly later than the orthodox tradition has it. His original name was Vardhamāna. Mahāvīra literally means 'great hero', and was a title bestowed upon him by his followers. The tradition asserts that his parents were followers of the teaching of Pārśva. His father was prince of a small state in Bihar, and Vardhamāna would have had an upbringing similar to that of the Buddha. He married a girl called Yaśodā, but at the age of thirty took to the life of an ascetic.

After twelve years of extreme self-denial he is said to have gained 'supreme knowledge', or kevala jnāna, after which he spent thirty years spreading his teaching. He is said to have abolished caste distinctions among his followers, although his closest disciples were all Brāhmins and one of the rules of his monks was that they should not take food if they had been touched by a Chandāla (a person of very low caste). Mahāvīra is regarded as the twenty-fourth Tīrthankara. He died, through self-starvation, a consequence of his extreme asceticism, at the age of seventy-two.

Jīva

The soul, or all that is spiritual or conscious. Jaina doctrine bears some resemblance to the Sāmkhya system. The soul is regarded as eternal, but enmeshed in matter which frustrates spiritual development and causes ignorance and suffering.

Ajīva

Non-soul. That which is unconscious or inanimate. Ajīva is what traps and and deludes the soul. The main aim of Jaina asceticism, therefore, is to gain liberation from the material world.

Kevalin

One who is complete, or whole, The title was accorded to Mahāvīra after his attainment of 'supreme knowledge'.

Ganadharas

The eleven chief disciples of Mahāvīra. Their names were: Indrabhūti, Agnibhūti, Vāyabhūti, Vyakta, Sudharman, Mandita, Moriyaputra, Akampita, Achalabhātā, Metārya, and Prabhāsa. They were all Brāhmins, although Jainas attribute this to the fact that Mahāvīra's teaching appealed to the intellectuals, rather than to any caste-exclusiveness in Jainism. Sudharman became the leader of the Jaina monks after the death of Mahāvīra, and a direct succession from these first disciples continued until 317 BC.

Nihnavas

Sects, of which there were seven in all, splitting on matters of doctrine from the organization begun by Mahāvīra The first Nihnava was started by Jamali during the lifetime of Mahāvīra.

Yati

The word means a 'striver', and was a name given to the Jaina monk. Mahāvīra organized his followers very effectively, and the lives of the Jaina monks were strictly regulated.

Shramana

The word generally refers to a class of wandering ascetics, much in evidence during the sixth century BC (see p. 57). But among Jainas the word was used for the novice monk.

Thera

The monk at the second stage of his life in the community. The Thera must have spent a few years as a monk and must be well versed in the scriptures.

Uvājjhāya (Upādhyāya)

A monk well versed in the twelve Angas, and capable of teaching them to the younger monks.

Ācharya (Arya)

The highest form of Jaina monk.

Vrata

A vow, or observance. Pārśva was said to have taught the necessity for the observance of four rules among the monks. Mahāvīra added a fifth. The five observances, when applied to monks, are known as Mahāvratas.

Ahimsā

Non-violence. This was a most important precept among the Jainas, and was taught by Pārśva as well as Mahāvīra. Āryan society had not been non-violent, and the Vedas depict the early Āryans as a warlike people who held military virtues in high regard. The innovation which ahimsā represented may be seen as a protest against the Brāhmin tradition of animal sacrifice. But it also illustrates the way in which Jaina teaching fostered or reflected new values which were to become very important in the Hindu tradition. Non-violence was taken to extremes by Jaina monks, who strained drinking water in order to avoid swallowing insects and swept the ground before them when they walked to avoid treading on living creatures. Some even refused to bathe because that might harm the vermin living on them.

Satya

Truthfulness. There is an etymological connection between the words for 'being' (sat) and 'truth' (satya) which has encouraged the view that truthfulness is an essential accompaniment of complete and harmonious living.

Asteya

Not stealing.

Aparigraha

Non-attachment to the world, sometimes interpreted as an injunction not to covet.

Brahmaçarya

Celibacy. This fifth vrata was added by Mahāvīra to the four that had been taught by Pārśva, although some Jainas maintain that for Pārśva aparigraha was understood to include chastity.

—

Shravaka

Literally a 'hearer', the term was used for the Jaina laymen. The layman is expected to observe twelve vows, which comprise a modified form of the five vows of the monk, plus: avoiding temptation by refraining from unnecessary travel; guarding against all evils; keeping specific times for meditation; imposing special periods of self-denial; spending occasional days as monks; giving alms in support of the monks; limiting the number of things in daily use.

Triratna

The 'three jewels': Right Faith, in the sense of a firm confidence in Jaina teaching; Right Knowledge, as a true understanding of Jaina principles; Right Conduct, based upon the vratas.

Itvara

Another example of Jaina asceticism is the practice of fasting. Itvara is temporary fasting.

Sallekhanā (Maranakāla)

Fasting to death. Mahāvīra was said to have ended his life through a self-imposed fast, and other Jaina monks have followed this extreme example of fasting.

Paramātman

Literally a 'great soul', the Paramātman for the Jaina is an accomplished Jaina who may become the object of veneration.

Gośāla

Gośāla was a companion of Mahāvīra for six years, before they parted over differences of belief. Gośāla founded a sect called the Ājīvikas, which survived until the fourteenth century. The cardinal point of Gośāla's teaching was belief in fate.

Āgama

A collective name for the sacred books of the Jainas. The word means 'manual' or 'code'. The canon of Jaina scriptures contains forty-five texts, and was finally approved at the Council of Valabhī in the fifth or sixth century CE.

Anga

'Anga' means limb, and in connection with Jaina scriptures refers to the twelve sections of scripture codified some two hundred years after the death of Mahāvīra.

Upānga

Twelve further secondary sections of scripture.

Tīrthankara

The word literally means 'one who makes a ford', and is used of the twenty-four great souls who are said to have preached the original Jaina doctrine. There is no historical basis for the lives of the first twenty-two; the twenty-third was Pārśva and the twenty-fourth Mahāvīra.

Chandragupta Maurya

A king of the Magadha dynasty who reigned from 317 until 293 BC. During his reign there was a great famine which was the cause of the migration of a large number of Jainas to South India.

Digambara

The 'sky-clad'. One of the two great sects of Jainas, whose name indicated that they followed the practice of nudity said to have been started by Mahāvīra. Nudity was an expression of the renunciation of attachment to things of the world. It appears to have been a common practice among Jainas at one time (many early statues of Tīrthankaras depict them naked) but it is now very little practised. Digambara monks have tended to a more extreme position in matters other than clothing, for in their history they have also been admonished to avoid baths and the cleaning of teeth.

Śvetāmbara

The 'white-clad'. The other main group, whose original distinction from the Digambara was that they wore a white cloth. The rift between the two groups was said to have occurred in 79 or 82 CE when monks from the group which had migrated south in the third century BC returned to the north to find their co-religionists there had, as they saw it, compromised on strict Jaina practice by adopting the wearing of a cloth. Śvetāmbara are still concentrated mostly in the north, and especially in Gujarāt, whilst the Digambara are to be found chiefly in Mysore.

Sthanakavasi

A sect which emerged out of Śvetāmbara in the early eighteenth century. The sect arose out of the insistence of a Jaina monk, Virāji, that Jainas should not permit temple or idol worship. In this he was probably influenced by the Muslim presence in India. The noun Sthanakavasi comes from sthanakas (buildings) and refers to the bare and unconsecrated buildings in which the members meet.

Syād-Vāda

The 'perhaps' method employed in Jaina philosophy. It expresses the notion that there is no certainty of any knowledge. To any proposition the answer has to be: Syād, maybe; syād-asti, perhaps it exists; Syād na-asti, perhaps it does not exist.

Paryushana

An act of penance undertaken on the last day of the Jaina year.

Raychandbhai (Raichand Bhai)

A great Jaina teacher of the nineteenth century who had a considerable influence on Mahatma Gāndhi.

Bibliography

A. L. Basham, 'Jainism' in *The Concise Encyclopaedia of Living Faiths*, R. C. Zaehner (ed.), 2nd ed., Hutchinson 1971
Bayanand Bhargava, *Jaina Ethics*, Motilal Banarsidas, Delhi 1968
Haripada Chakraborty, *Asceticism in Ancient India in Brahmanical, Buddhist, Jaina and Ajivika Societies*, Punthi Pustak, Calcutta 1973
S. Gopalan, *Outlines of Jainism*, Wiley Eastern Private Ltd, New Delhi 1973
Muni Uttam Kamal Jain, *Jaina Sects and Schools*, Concept Publishing Company, Delhi 1975
J. Jaini, *Outlines of Jainism*, Cambridge University Press 1916, University Microfilms 1972
R. C. Majumdar, H. C. Rayachaudhuri and K. Datta, *An Advanced History of India*, 2nd ed., Macmillan 1950

8 Buddhism

Buddhism arose in India in the sixth century BC. The origins of what was to become one of the world's greatest religions were related to cultural and economic changes in North India at the time, and to movements which questioned the prevailing Brāhmanism. The Jainas were influencing Indian religion by their ascetic practices and extreme attitudes on non-violence, celibacy and diet. Their influence was to have a profound affect upon Hinduism in some of its later developments.

Buddhism also questioned Brāhmanism in the sixth century, and rejected the contemporary concern with a religion in which sacrifice and ritual played an important part and in which the Brāhmin was indispensable. But Buddhism offered a different answer from that of the Jainas. Original Buddhism appears to have been a radical movement in its rejection of many of the accepted religious and social customs of the day and in its indifference to some basic religious questions.

Its radical nature was seen partly in its rejection of caste. The Buddha was a Kshatriya, not a Brāhmin, and the Sangha as it developed was open to men of all castes. On traditional religious questions Buddhism was often agnostic, and the Buddha is said to have refused to discuss such metaphysical questions as, 'Is there a God?'

Buddhism originated in the far north of India, and in its early years was associated with the growing urban centres which developed in the north Gangetic plain on the trade routes between the north-west and the south-east. The growth of these towns marked a shift from the earlier village-based communities of India, and was accompanied by the rise of a prosperous merchant class. Some scholars have regarded this change in the socio-economic structure as a significant factor in the growth of Buddhism. Trevor Ling, for example, regards early Buddhism as an attempt to answer new questions which arose with the increasing individualism of life in the town.[1]

[1]See Trevor Ling, *The Buddha*, Penguin 1976, chs. 3–4.

The Buddha was a member of a princely family in the Sakya country of North India. He is said to have been greatly concerned by the suffering he saw around him, and it was to solve the problems of human pain and misery and dissatisfaction that he set out on his quest for truth. The Buddha first attempted to follow the methods of traditional Indian ascetics, but after six years he realized that he was not making spiritual progress. He abandoned his ascetic life-style and almost immediately gained 'enlightenment'. Then he began to teach others what he had discovered. The 'Four Noble Truths' enunciated his ideas of the links between human desire or craving, suffering, and dissatisfaction with life. An essential part of Buddhist thought is its teaching about the impermanence of everything upon which people normally depend. All life is suffering because nothing that we cling to for pleasure or security can last. We are constantly changing, and everything around us is in a state of change. So not only is life threatened by disease, wasting, old age and death, but even our pleasures are marred by their transience. Nothing lasts. Our closest relationships, our dearest possessions and our most cherished achievements all disintegrate with the passage of time. Faced by this truth of the impermanence of all things, the person who seeks peace must learn to 'let go' of his craving for passing joys.

Among the significant features of early Buddhism were its rejection of caste and sacrifice, both of which were very important in the Brahmanical religion of the time. Original Buddhism was not concerned with God or with worship; it concentrated upon personal understanding and social reform. Later Buddhism, however, developed more traditional religious forms.

Buddhism flourished for many centuries in India. It spread to Śri Lanka and other parts of South-East Asia, where the Theravāda form of Buddhism has predominated. Early in the Christian era the Mahāyāna school of Buddhism spread northwards into China, Korea, Japan and Tibet. In China and Japan Buddhism developed new forms, the best -known of which in the West today is Zen Buddhism. In India Buddhism eventually declined and virtually disappeared from the country of its birth. This is thought to have been partially due to Hindu opposition, although the final death-blow to Buddhism in India was dealt by Muslim invaders in the thirteenth century. By that time there had been a certain amount of absorption of Buddhist ideas into Hinduism.

Unlike Hinduism, Buddhism has always been a missionary religion, eager to disseminate its teaching. In recent years the coming of independence and the rise of nationalism in many Buddhist countries has been accompanied by a renewed emphasis upon the message Buddhism has for the non-Buddhist world. In 1950 a World

Buddhist Fellowship was founded 'to strive to make known the
sublime doctrine of the Buddha, so that its benign spirit of service
and sacrifice may pervade the entire world'. Buddhist monks are now
active in Europe and the USA as well as in Asia.

Buddha

The title of the founder of Buddhism. The word means 'the
enlightened one', and is from a root meaning 'to awaken, become
conscious'. Although the title is usually used of the founder of
Buddhism, there is a widespread belief that there have been, and will
be, many Buddhas. The Buddha did not claim to be other than a
human being who had discovered enlightenment. His discovery led
him to teach the ideal of the 'Middle Way', a path to enlightenment
which avoided the extremes of asceticism and sensual enjoyment.

Gautama (Gotama)

The family name of the Buddha. His father, Suddhodana, was the
ruler of the Sākya country at the foot of the Himālayas and on the
borders of the present Indian State of Uttar Pradesh and Nepal. The
Buddha is sometimes known as Sākyamuni (the wise man of the
Sākyas). His father eventually became a convert to Buddhism, as did
his son.

Siddhārtha

The personal name of the Buddha. He was born at Lumbini, near
Kapilavastu, probably in 563 BC (the date is disputed). As the son of a
local ruler, he had a sheltered upbringing. He was married at the age
of sixteen. When he was twenty-nine, Siddhārtha left home to
become a wandering ascetic. He is said to have been troubled by
thoughts of disease, old age, and death, and so by the impermanence
of the pleasures of life. For six years he practised severe austerities,
in the company of other ascetics. Only after this did he come to the
discovery of the 'Middle Way'.

Kapilavastu

The early home of Siddhārtha. Kapilavastu lies on the trade routes
running north-west to south-east between the Gangetic plain and the
Himālayas, and it shared in the expansion of urban areas which was a
feature of North India at the time of the Buddha.

Māyā

The mother of Siddhārtha, who died seven days after the birth of her
son.

Yaśodharā

The wife of Siddhārtha who lived for thirteen years with her husband before he left her and his home in his search for enlightenment.

Rāhula

Siddhārtha's son. It was just after the birth of Rāhula that Siddhārtha left home. Rāhula can mean 'a bond', and this has led some commentators to suggest that Siddhārtha saw in the birth of his son another example of the 'bondage' to the world that appeared to cause suffering.

Shramana

A mendicant philosopher. Shramanas were common in the India of the sixth century BC. They gathered their own followers and formed their own sects. They were mostly non-Brāhmins, and rejected the authority of the Vedas and the caste system. The Buddha was regarded by some as a Shramana (see pp. 49 f.).

Bodhi Tree

The tree of awakening, or enlightenment. After years of ascetic practice which did not lead to the desired spiritual progress, Siddhārtha abandoned his great austerities. The five other ascetics who had been his companions left him in disgust. According to Buddhist tradition Siddhārtha then sat under a peepal tree at Bodh Gaya for seven days in meditation, and then awoke to the truth. So the tree which witnessed his enlightenment was called the Bodhi tree.

Tathāgata

A title of the Buddha, the word means 'one who has succeeded'.

Upaka

A man of the Ājīvika sect (see p. 51) who, according to Mahāvagga, a Buddhist text, was the first to greet the Buddha after his awakening. Buddha told Upaka: 'I have overcome all foes. I am all-wise'. This direct connection between the Buddha and an ascetic sect of the time illustrates the way in which varied experiments which differed from the prevailing Brāhmanism contributed to each other and to the development of Indian religion during the sixth century BC.

Sārnāth

A place near Varanāsi where the Buddha preached his first sermon to the five ascetics who had previously been his companions. They then became his first followers.

The ancient name of the place was Isipatana.

Dhammacakkappavattana Sutta

The title of the Buddha's first sermon, it means 'the discourse which set the wheel of truth turning'. It is said to have contained basic teaching about the Middle Way.

Fire Sermon (Ādityaparyāya Sutta)

A sermon preached at Gayā to one thousand Jatilas, or fire-worshipping ascetics, who became disciples of the Buddha. He agreed with them about the importance of fire and burning, but then asked them, 'With what is everything burning?' The answer he provided was 'Everything burns with the fires of lust and anger and ignorance'.

Upasake

A lay follower of the Buddha, who did not wish or was not able to abandon life in the world for a life totally within the Sangha. The Upasake, however, associated himself as closely as possible with the Sangha, and observed the five vows which were required of the lay Buddhist. The vows prohibit violence, theft, lying, the use of alcohol, and illicit sexual relationships.

Arhat (Arahant)

The ideal of the Sthavira school of Buddhism, the Arhat is a Buddhist who gains his own enlightenment by following the path of orthodox Buddhism laid down in the Vinaya. The word means 'one who is worthy'.

The Four Holy Places

The four places associated with the most significant stages of the life of the Buddha: in the grounds of Lumbinī, his birth; at Bodh Gayā, his enlightenment; at Varanāsi, his first sermon; at Kuśinagara, his death.

9   Buddhist belief and practice

The Middle Way

A name given to the teaching of the Buddha, who endeavoured to strike a mean between the excesses of self-indulgence and the excesses of self-denial.

Dhamma

The Pali form of Dharma (Sanskrit). Dhamma is applied to the whole teaching of the Buddha, as well as more generally to right conduct and cosmic law.

Pali

The religious language of Buddhism, Pali was one of the Prakrit vernaculars of North India at the time of the Buddha. Pali has many words in common with Sanskrit, although there are often differences in spelling. Pali was a simpler language than the Sanskrit used by the Brāhmins.

Triratna

The word means 'three jewels', and refers to the basic affirmation of the Buddhist: 'I take refuge in the Buddha; I take refuge in the Dhamma; I take refuge in the Sangha.'

Tisarana

The taking of the three refuges, in the Buddha, the Dhamma, and the Sangha.

Śraddhā

Faith, in the sense of confidence that there is a goal to be reached and that Buddhist practice will lead to it.

Bhikkhu

The Buddhist 'monk', although this is a somewhat misleading synonym, since the Bhikkhu's life is not essentially one lived apart from other people. It is, rather, a life devoted to exploring and practising the principles of Buddhism. The word bhikkhu means 'one who shares', and is derived from the share of food and other resources given by the householder for the support of the bhikkhus. The close relationship between the laity and the lives of the bhikkhus is a significant element in Buddhism.

The bhikkhu is allowed few possessions. He may have three garments (an inner garment, an outer garment, and a cloak), a bowl for food, a filter for his water, a razor, a toothpick, a needle, stick, and fan. The food which the bhikkhu is given should be eaten by midday.

In the early years of Buddhism the bhikkhus spent much of their time wandering the country, and gathered in temporary shelters during the rainy season. Gradually the shelters assumed greater proportions, and the bhikkhus came to live most of their time in monasteries which were centres of learning as well as of spiritual life.

Bhikkhuni

After what appears to have been a long period of prohibition, the Buddha relented in the face of many demands from women to enter the Buddhist order. They were allowed to become bhikkhuni, and were given twice as many rules to obey as the men.

Sangha

The community of those Buddhists who leave their homes and families in order to become bhikkhus. The sangha is said to have originated when the Buddha addressed a gathering of his disciples soon after his enlightenment, saying to them: 'Go now, monks, and wander for the gain of many, out of compassion for the world, for the good, for the gain, for the welfare of gods and men.' The sangha has always been of great importance in Buddhism.

The vows taken upon entry to the sangha are not irrevocable. Whilst many become bhikkhus and remain within the sangha for the rest of their lives, there are others who live in the sangha for a time and then return to the ordinary life of the world. It is possible to enter the monastery at as young an age as eight years, and many boys in Buddhist countries spend some time in a monastery. Full entry to the community is from the age of twenty.

On entering the sangha the bhikkhu has his head shaved and adopts the wearing of a yellow, or saffron, robe. In addition to the five prohibitions of the lay Buddhist, the bhikkhu is expected to observe five extra precepts. These are: not eating outside the prescribed times; not taking part in or being present at entertainments; not using perfumes; not using a too comfortable bed; not handling gold or silver. In recent times some of the these prohibitions have been found to be impracticable and have been relaxed.

Pravrajyā

This literally means 'going forth', and is a ceremonial which marks the bhikkhu's formal entry into the community.

Shrāmanera

The novice monk after Pravrajyā and before ordination. When this period is satisfactorily completed, the bhikkhu is ordained. It is the time and place of ordination that determines the place of a bhikkhu in the strict order of seniority.

Uposatha

An act of public confession which takes place in the sangha twice a month for a day each time.

Vihāra

A place of rest and retreat for bhikkhus. Originally this was a simple shelter, but the vihāra developed into the monastery of later times (see p. 67).

Vinaya

The code of discipline for bhikkhus, set out in the Vinayapitaka.

Buddha Sāsana

The fundamental injunctions (sāsana) of the Buddhist religion. The sāsana includes the celebrated words: 'Abstain from all evil, learn to do good, and purify your mind—this is the teaching of all the Buddhas'.

The Four Noble Truths

A summary of the Buddha's teaching:
1. All life is suffering (dukkha); even pleasure contains the seeds of suffering within it.
2. The cause of suffering is desire or craving; we try to hold on to what by their nature are impermanent things.
3. Suffering can be eliminated only when desire is extingushed.
4. The way to overcome desire is to employ the method of the eightfold path.

The Eightfold Path

Sammā ditthi

Right understanding, which involves seeing through delusions such as the idea that material possessions can bring peace or that rituals and ceremonies can help.

Sammā sankappa

Right motives. This includes rooting out wrong motives and cultivating such qualities as unselfishness, generosity, compassion, and insight.

Sammā vācā

Right speech. Not indulging in gossip or lying, and using conversation as a means of understanding other people.

Sammā kammanta

Right action, which is more than simply obeying the precepts. It demands the avoidance of bad karma.

Sammā ajīva

Right means of livelihood. This suggests that the Buddhist should find some means of livelihood which is conducive to his spiritual growth, and should avoid occupations that involve breaking the five precepts.

Sammā vāyāma

Right effort. This involves the effort of ridding oneself of unwholesome states of mind and of cultivating what is conducive to spiritual growth. It requires insight, intuition, and will-power.

Sammā sati

Right mindfulness. The Buddhist should be mindful, or aware, of his body, his feelings, and his mind, and this awareness should be related to Buddhist teaching generally.

Sammā samādhi

Right concentration, or meditation.

—

Anicca

Impermanence. A basic part of Buddhist teaching is that all phenomena are subject to change. Nothing remains the same, and so it is futile to depend upon anything in the phenomenal world. Man, his body, his mind, his 'self', his relationships, are all constantly changing. A large part of our suffering is due to our clinging to what cannot possibly last; in order to reach enlightenment we have to 'let go'.

Dukkha

A basic tenet of Buddhist teaching is that all life involves suffering. Birth, illness, decay, death, all involve suffering. Even the apparently pleasant experiences of life contain the prospect of suffering, for they cannot last. A large part of suffering is due to the desire for permanence in a world which is impermanent.

Anatta

Literally 'non-self'. The idea of non-individuality clearly distinguishes Buddhist from Hindu teaching. The idea of a soul which passes from one life to another as a permanent entity was rejected by Buddhism. Even the self is not permanent, but like other parts of the phenomenal world is a constant flux. So the Buddhist is taught to 'let go' of the self as well as of the phenomenal world in order to find enlightenment.

Paticcasamuppāda

The cycle of causation, by which one life is linked to the next, a chain made up of ignorance, craving, and thirst which binds people to the wheel of suffering.

Nibbāna (Nirvāna)

Nibbāna (the Pali form: Nirvāna is Sanskrit) expresses an important but subtle Buddhist idea. Nibbāna is the state in which suffering no longer occurs, and all afflictions are extinguished. The idea that Nibbāna is annihilation or extinction was expressly repudiated by the Buddha. Nibbāna, it is said, is a state of peace and happiness reached by the extinction of craving and desire. Many images have been used in order to express what is meant by Nibbāna – the island amidst the floods, the harbour of refuge, the supreme bliss, the immortal.

Khanda (Skandha)

Khandha (Sanskrit – Skandha) refers to a group of five factors which make up the human personality. They are continuously changing and restructuring according to the action of karma. They are: Rūpa, or form. The material or physical aspect of human personality. Vedanā, or sense perception. Sannā, or consciousness. Sankhāra, or (Samskāra) intellectual faculties. Vinnāna, or discrimination.

Tanhā

Grasping or craving. The desire to hold on to things which is at the root of most of the suffering of man.

Dāna

Giving. Developing the will to give is one of the most important of the 'wholesome states' of Buddhism.

Metta

Loving-kindness or compassion. Metta is the feeling of concern for others at least equal to one's self-concern. Ideally, the Buddhist should be equally compassionate towards all people.

Kamma

The Pali form of 'karma'. The action or deeds which accumulate to determine the destiny of man. In spite of the Anatta doctrine, Buddhists retained a belief in kamma.

Vipāka
The effect of past kamma.

Kusala
Akusala
These are two types of consciousness. Kusala are actions useful for personal liberation, and akusala are actions which are not conducive to personal liberation.

10 Buddhist scriptures

Tipitaka
The 'triple basket', which is the canonical scripture for Theravāda Buddhists. The Tipitaka is written in Pali. The first form of the canon is said to have been accepted at the Council of Rājagriha immediately after the death of the Buddha. Further development took place at the second Buddhist Council, at Vesāli, and the final form, including the addition of the Abhidhammapitaka, was evidently in existence by the time of the third Council held during the reign of Ashoka. The three component parts of the Tipitaka are the Vinayapitaka, the Suttapitaka, and the Abhidhammapitaka.

Vinayapitaka
A collection of sayings attributed to the Buddha and containing rules and guidance for bhikkhus and for the life of the sangha. It also contains an account of the origins of Buddhism.

Suttapitaka
The second basket consists of five collections of writings:
1. **Dīgha Nikāya**   A collection of sermons attributed to the Buddha.
2. **Majjhima Nikāya**   A collection of shorter sermons.
3. **Samyutta Nikāya**   A collection of short sayings.

4. **Anguttara Nikāya** A collection of over 2,000 brief statements, mostly on doctrinal subjects.

5. **Khuddaka Nikāya** A collection of miscellaneous prose and verse, including the Dhammapada (verses on Dhamma) and the Jataka Tales (some 500 folk stories in verse form).

Abhidhamma
The third basket consists of systematic accounts of the teaching of various schools, mostly couched in the form of commentaries on the Suttas.

Milinda Panha
An extra-canonical work, also known as 'The Questions of King Menander'. It is in the form of a discussion on Buddhism between the Greco-Bactrian king Menander and a Buddhist bhikkhu, Nāgasena.

11 The development of Buddhism in India

Shravasti
One of six important cities of the Ganges plain at the time of the Buddha, when the urban centres were growing in importance. Shravasti was the capital of the Koshala kingdom, a trading centre through which many caravans passed, and the home of wealthy merchants. According to some scholars (especially Ling) an important element in the rise of Buddhism was the need to answer the new questions posed by the increase of city life. Prefaces to Buddhist texts indicate that much of the Buddha's teaching was given at Shravasti and Rājagriha.

Rājagriha
The capital of the Magadhan kingdom in what is now Bihar. Rājagriha was also a centre for trade, and it appears to have been a prosperous city. In this and other cities of the Gangetic plain the growth of trade, of a merchant class, and of the monarchy all

contributed to the development of the great urban centres. Rājagriha is also the place where a gathering of bhikkhus was held after the death of the Buddha. Two disciples expounded the rules and teaching they were to follow. Upāli recited the Vinayapitaka, the rules governing the life of the sangha, and Ānanda recited the Suttapitaka, a collection of Buddha's sermons. So began the formulation of Buddhist scriptures.

Chandragupta Maurya

A king of Magadha from 317 until 293 BC (see p. 52).

Devi

The first wife of Chandragupta. The family appear to have been influenced by Jaina belief, but some were also attracted to Buddhism. Devi's two children by the king, Mahinda and Sanghamitra, are said to have entered the sangha as bhikkhu and bhikkhuni.

Ashoka (Aśoka)

The grandson of Chandragupta, and the first great Buddhist emperor, Ashoka ruled from about 270 – 232 BC. He ruled at first according to the conventions of statecraft outlined by Chandragupta's Brāhmin adviser, Kautilya. His early military successes led him to become emperor of most of India, with the exception of the southern Tamil country. But after a great (and successful) war against the state of Kalinga, Ashoka became a Buddhist. He gave up the pursuit of conquest by force of arms, and advocated conquest by moral example. He undertook lengthy tours of his kingdom to speak about dhamma and morality. He abolished the sacrificial slaughter of animals, and ended or strictly limited the killing of animals for food. He also abolished the Royal Hunt.

Ashoka's example did much to foster the spread of Buddhism throughout India and beyond. But by the time of his death his empire was being eroded by invasions from the north-west.

Rock Edicts

Ashoka promulgated his policies after his conversion to Buddhism by the means of edicts which he had engraved on rocks and pillars throughout the country. The edicts were written in Prakrit, and gave general moral advice. They provide indications of the ways in which Buddhism influenced Ashoka in the running of his empire.

Stupa

A mound associated with sacred places or relics in Buddhism. It is possible that the stupa represented an earlier religious custom which was adopted by Buddhism. The practice of enshrining relics in a stupa was an indication of the development of popular religious aspects, including worship, in Buddhism. Many stupas appear to have been erected during the time of Ashoka. It was regarded as a great act of merit for a layman to erect a stupa.

Lena

The word means 'a private dwelling-place', and refers to Buddhist monasteries as places for a settled community rather than shelters for wandering bhikkhus. The two types of lenas are the vihāra and the guhā.

Vihāra

(See p. 61). The earliest vihāras were simply huts for the bhikkhus to live in for temporary periods, but they developed into buildings which served both as monasteries for the sangha and as places of worship and pilgrimage for the laity. The vihāra was found chiefly in North India.

Guhā

Buddhist monasteries built of rock, and found chiefly in Central and South India. More remains of these have survived than of the vihāra. Among the best-known survivals of the rock-dwellings are Ellorā and Ajantā.

Nālandā

The most famous of the centres of Buddhist learning in India, Nālandā developed from a monastery into a university. As well as teaching Buddhism, it offered instruction in the Vedas, Logic, Grammar, and Hindu Philosophy. It endured until the Muslim invasion, and was destroyed by Muslims in the thirteenth century CE. It was situated close to Rājagriha on the north-west – south-east trade route, and attracted students from all over India and far beyond.

Sthaviras

Literally this means 'the elders'. It was a party of conservative Buddhists which emerged at the Second Buddhist Council at Vesāli, some hundred years after the death of the Buddha. The Sthaviras held strictly to the rules of the Vināya. The origins of the Theravāda are found in this school.

Mahāsanghikās

The Great Sangha party, which adopted a more liberal attitude towards the rules for the sangha. The Mahāsanghikas gave greater importance to the role of the laity in Buddhism, and emphasized the importance of meditation. They also emerged at the Council of Vesāli. In this school are to be found the seeds of the Mahāyāna.

Vibhajyavādins
A school of philosophy within Buddhism which emerged in the third century BC. Little is known about them, except that they were concerned with the processes of logical analysis.

Sarvastivādins
A school which arose midway through the second century BC, and held that past and future dhammas have real consequences for the present. They were strong in the regions of Kashmir and Mathurā.

Pudgalavādins
A school which arose at the end of the fourth century BC. Contrary to the main strand of Buddhist teaching, they asserted that there is a person (pudgala) or self which endures through reincarnations. This appears to have been an accommodation to the Hindu concept of the self, in contrast with the 'not-self' doctrine, and to Hindu ideas of karma and transmigration.

Pātaliputra (Patna)
The place where the Third Buddhist Council was held, under the patronage of Ashoka. It was here that the final form of the Pali canon (the Vinayapitaka, Suttapitaka and Abhidhammapitaka) was agreed. The Council also agreed to send bhikkhus to neighbouring countries, especially Śri Lanka.

12 Mahāyāna Buddhism

Mahābheda
The great schism between the Sthaviras and the Mahāsanghikās (see p. 67) which foreshadowed the breach between Theravāda and Mahāyāna Buddhism.

Hīnayāna

The 'lesser vehicle', a name given to the orthodox school of early Buddhism by the Mahāyānists. The name implied that the earlier form of Buddhism was a more difficult and restricted path to enlightenment than Mahāyāna. Hīnayāna related to the Sthavira school, and used the language of Pali.

Theravāda

Theravāda means 'the teaching of the elders', and claims that it represents the orthodox teaching of the original Buddhist canon. The Theravāda was one of the eighteen sects of Hīnayāna. Most of the others have long since disappeared, but Theravāda has flourished in South-East Asia, and is now the prevalent form of Buddhism in Śri Lanka, Malaysia, Thailand and Cambodia.

Mahāyāna

Mahāyāna developed the ideas of the Mahāsanghikā school. The name, 'The Great Vehicle', implies that Mahāyāna is a more popular form of Buddhism than Hīnayāna, and that it offers a more comprehensive system than the older school. In spite of the name, however, Mahāyāna remained a minority movement in Indian Buddhism until 500 CE. Mahāyāna appears to have developed first in North-West and South India, and this, together with some of the features of Mahāyāna, has led to the suggestion that foreign and possibly Christian elements played a part in the development of Mahāyāna.

Mahāyāna has given greater attention to the role of the layman in Buddhism, and proportionately less emphasis has been placed upon the bhikkhu's role. Ideas and practices were developed in Mahāyāna which were more in accord with popular religious sentiment than Hīnayāna. It was within Mahāyāna that popular devotion to Buddhas developed, worship became a normal part of religion, and there was even introduced a saviour figure into Buddhism. Mahāyāna spread northwards out of India, and provided the predominant forms of Buddhism in Nepal, China, Tibet, Korea, and Japan.

Buddha-rūpa

The 'form of the Buddha'. Buddha-rūpas are statues, the remains of the earliest of which have been found in North-West India. They indicate the way in which the Buddha came to be thought of as a divine being in Mahāyāna Buddhism.

Bodhisattva

One of the distinctive and important contributions of Mahāyāna to Buddhism was in the idea of the Bodhisattva. The idea originated in the Mahāsanghikā, but was developed in Mahāyāna. The Bodhisattva represents a kind of saviour figure. He is regarded as an enlightened being (bodhi is 'enlightenment'; sattva is 'being') who postpones his own enjoyment of the bliss of nibbāna in order to help others along the path. In the Mahāyana there were thought to be ten stages through which the bodhisattva must pass on his way to nibbāna. At the sixth stage nibbāna is open to him, and it is then that he voluntarily relinquishes it. After this he is miraculously reborn to help others.

Saddharmapundarīka

The Lotus of the Good Law. Mahāyāna made use of the scriptures of the Pali canon but added much material of its own. The Lotus of the Good Law is a well-known additional text which provides a fairly clear exposition of the major ideas of Mahāyāna. Mahāyāna used the language of Sanskrit instead of Pali, and there is some evidence that the use of Sanskrit was part of a wider accommodation to the religion of the Brāhmins.

Mādhyamika

A school of Mahāyāna Buddhism founded by Nāgārjuna in the second century CE. Mādhyamika means 'middle position', and it was regarded as a school which stood between the Sarvāstivadins, for whom all dhammas are real, and the Yogācarins, who take a position of absolute idealism. The school was also known as the sūnyavādin. It asserted that all things are without substance; even dhammas (which the Theravādins regarded as being possessed of ultimate reality) have no permanent substance. On the relationship between the phenomenal world and nibbāna the Mādhyamika taught that nibbāna is present, although unrecognized, within the world of samsāra. But to know the presence of nibbāna, the Buddhists has to acknowledge the insubstantial nature of the things of the world.

Yogācāra

The other main philosophical school of Mahāyāna, Yogācāra is thought to have been founded by Maitreyaratha in the third century CE. It was developed considerably during the fourth century by Asanga and Vāsubandhu. It emphasized the practice of meditation (a yogācāra is one who practises meditation). The school is also known as vijnānavāda because of its assertion that only consciousness (vijnāna) is real. External objects are said to exist only through the action of consciousness.

Mahinda

A son of Ashoka and a bhikkhu, Mahinda was sent to Śri Lanka where he established a Buddhist community. This community was the forerunner of the Mahāvihāra, which was the main Buddhist sect of Śrī Lanka for a long period. The island of Lanka has remained one of the leading centres of Theravāda Buddhism.

Buddhaghosa
A celebrated bhikkhu and scholar of the Lanka Theravāda school, Buddhaghosa lived in the fourth to fifth centuries CE. He wrote commentaries on the Pali canon and a major work called Visuddhimagga (the Path of Purification).

---

13 Buddhism in China

Han Dynasty
Mahāyāna Buddhism passed from North-West India into Central Asia around the second century CE and then gradually moved along the trade routes into Western China. Dates and details of the establishment of Buddhism in China are uncertain, but it seems to have been established, at least among foreigners, as the Han dynasty declined in the second century CE. However, there was also influence exerted by the Hīnayāna school from the beginnings of Buddhism in China. Hīnayānist texts, translated from Sanskrit, were particularly influential on monastic discipline and the meditation schools. Taoist scholars assisted with the translations of Buddhist texts, and so Buddhism was sometimes conveyed through Taoist terms.

Kumārajīva
A Buddhist monk who lived from 344 until 413. He arrived at Ch'ang-an, in China, in 401, and is said to have translated more than one hundred texts into Chinese. His translation work was of great importance for the propagation of Buddhism in China and for the serious consideration of Buddhist philosophy alongside Chinese thought.

Tao-an
A Buddhist monk who did much for the development of Buddhism in

China in the mid-fourth century CE. He established a centre of Buddhist learning in northern Hupei. As well as giving an important place to intellectual Buddhism, he stressed the values of devotional Buddhism, especially the cult of Maitreya.

Period of Disunity

The period from 220 until 589 CE, which was a time of acclimatization and great development for Chinese Buddhism. Great monasteries were founded, the Vinaya rules were established, and the great speculative ideas of the Mahāyāna were widely disseminated. Important Buddhist figures of this period were Tao-an (312–385), Hui Yüan (344–416), and Tao-sheng. Tao-sheng expounded the doctrine that all men possess the Buddha nature, and for this he was attacked by the older monks and expelled from the sangha. But later, when the Nirvāna Sūtra was translated, his views were vindicated.

Fa Hsien

A famous Buddhist pilgrim to India in 399 CE. His journey inspired other pilgrims, and visits to Buddhist centres in India became an important source of inspiration for Chinese Buddhism.

Hsuan Chung

Probably the most celebrated of the Chinese Buddhist pilgrims to India, Hsüan Chuang lived from 596 until 664 CE. He spent thirteen years in India, and on his return to China was greeted with great acclaim. He engaged in extensive works of translation, and had a considerable influence on Chinese Buddhism.

T'ang Dynasty

The T'ang Dynasty lasted from 618 until 907 CE, and on the whole was favourable to Buddhism. During this period Chinese Buddhism reached the peak of its influence. Many Chinese Buddhists visited India to see the sacred places of Buddhism and to study at such places as Nālandā. Monasteries in China became even more plentiful, and a powerful influence in society. They provided medical care and other welfare services.

Wu Tsung

An emperor (from 841 until 847) under whom Buddhism suffered severe persecution. In 843 there was a campaign against the Christian Manichaeists, and in 845 this was followed by a persecution of Buddhists. An imperial decree ordered the dismantling of the sangha and the confiscation of its lands and property. A census taken in 845 had revealed that there were a quarter of a million monks and nuns and nearly five thousand Buddhist temples in China, and this appears to have provoked a reaction which was encouraged by Taoist priests. By this time China had become much more isolated from the rest of the world, and was separated from western and southern Asia by Islam.

An unintended result of the persecution was the increase in the printing of the scriptures. It was during the eighth century CE that printing techniques had been invented in China, and this aided the production of Buddhist scriptures. A copy of the Diamond Sūtra, printed in 868, is the oldest surviving printed book in the world.

However, Chinese Buddhism never fully recovered from the persecution of this period.

Buddhas and Bodhisattvas

The historical Buddha, often refereed to as Sākyamuni, is commonly regarded as a transcendental saviour in Chinese Buddhism. Many images of Sākyamuni are to be found in Chinese art, and in some sects he is regarded as an object of worship.

Amitābha

A former Bodhisattava (see pp. 69 f.) who is thought of as presiding over the 'Pure Land' of Sukāvatī in the West. Amitābha is thought to have accumulated unlimited merit, and from his store to bestow merit upon those who call on his name. Full enlightenment is believed to be possible through the grace of Amitābha.

Bhaisjyagura Buddha

Literally 'the master of healing', he is believed to be able to cure illnesses and avert disasters. To invoke his aid his followers were invited to call upon his name and to recite the Bhaisjyagura Sutra.

Avalokiteśvara

A Bodhisattva who is regarded as being full of compassion and active help towards men. In China, where Avalokiteśvara was known as Kuan-yin, or Kwan-yin, this Bodhisattva was sometimes thought of as female, and the goddess of mercy. In accordance with the popular idea of Buddhist rulers being incarnations of Bodhisattvas, Avalokiteśvara is thought to be reincarnated as the Dalai Lama of Tibet.

Kshitigarbha

A Bodhisattva who is especially concerned with rescuing people from hell.

Maitreya (Mettayya)

Maitreya is the future Buddha who is thought to reside in the Tushita heaven. In some areas the concept of Maitreya has sometimes led to the idea of a coming saviour.

Sects and Schools in Chinese Buddhism

San Lun

A school which arose around 400 CE. The name means 'three treatises' and the school is based upon three Mādhyamika texts translated by Kumārajīva.

Fa-hsiang

A school which arose around 650 CE, based upon the teaching of the Yogācārins.

T'ien t'ai

T'ien t'ai was founded by Chi-I in the sixth century CE. Its philosophy is a combination of Mādhyamika and Vijnānavāda, and it also teaches the yogic insights of correct posture and breathing and meditation. The chief scripture of the school is the Lotus Sutta.

Hua-Yen

'The Garland School' was founded by Tu-Shun (557–640) and brought to completion by Fa-tsang (643–712). This school prohibited meat-eating, and its example was to become common practice among Chinese monks.

Chen-Yen

The Chinese version of Mantrayāna, Chen-Yen is a form of Tantric Buddhism. It was introduced into China about 720 CE. Chen-Yen practice consists of contemplating symbolic representations of the chief Buddhas and Bodhisattvas, and it generally made much use of mantras (short verses rhythmically repeated) and mudras (symbolic positioning of the hands and fingers). The school also had a rite of initiation.

Chin T'u (Pure Land)

One of the greatest and most enduring sects of modern Buddhism, the Pure Land sect arose in the fourth century CE and focused attention upon devotion to Amitābha. The founder is believed to have been Hui-Yüan, although the most famous leader of the sect was Shan-tao (613–681). Shan-tao distinguished two paths to enlightenment: through one's own efforts (the way of early Buddhism), and through reliance upon Amitābha's grace. But in degenerate times, he suggested, only the second of these was practicable. So he taught the need for absolute reliance upon the grace bestowed by Amitābha. Some suggest that in its formative stages the sect may have been influenced by Nestorian Christianity.

Ch'an

The word Ch'an is derived from the Sanskrit dhyāna (meditation), although the most significant part of this school is its emphasis upon sudden enlightenment. Ch'an represents an original Chinese contribution to Buddhism which has had lasting importance. It developed further in Japan, and under its Japanese name of Zen this school has attracted much attention in the West.

Ch'an showed signs of impatience with contemporary forms of Buddhist practice which concentrated on the role of the bhikkhu and the lengthy and formal discipline of the monastery. Ch'an, by contrast, aimed at instantaneous enlightenment.

Bodhidharma

Said to have been the first teacher of Ch'an. He was a monk who went to China from South India early in the sixth century CE. Bodhidharma introduced the sharp questioning of accepted values and teaching (including those of Buddhism) and the use of startling paradoxes which have been the hallmarks of Ch'an and Zen. It is said that when Bodhidharma arrived at the Imperial Court the Emperor asked him how much merit he had accumulated by his building of monasteries and his support of the bhikkhus. 'No merit at all', replied Bodhidharma. 'What is the absolute truth?' the Emperor asked. 'Great emptiness' was the reply.

In the seventh century there was a division of Ch'an into distinct schools. The southern school, led by Hui-neng, taught the idea of realization by the sudden apprehension of truth.

Ch'an retained the monastic system, but required the bhikkhus to engage in physical labour (an idea introduced by Po-chang, who lived from 720 until 814). This kind of work for the bhikkhu was made possible by the Ch'an practice of giving the monk a single verse to concentrate upon or by the mental discipline of the koan (see p. 78). A summary of Ch'an in famous lines which are attributed to Bodhidharma defines the system thus: a special transmission of truth outside the scriptures; no dependence on words or letters; a direct pointing to the soul of man; seeing directly into the nature and attainment of Buddhahood.

Hui-neng (638–713)

Hui-neng is the reputed author of the Platform Sūtra, the only Chinese work to achieve the status of 'ching' or 'sūtra'. During his time Ch'an divided. The northern school, led by Shen-hsiu, taught the need to eliminate false thinking and to cultivate quiet. The southern school, led by Hui-neng, stressed sudden enlightenment.

Tripitaka (San Tsang)

The basic Chinese Buddhist scriptures are often referred to as the Tripitaka, and are also known by the Chinese name of San Tsang. Two-thirds of the Chinese Tripitaka consists of translations from Indian scriptures. The remainder is made up of Chinese additions. The two largest sections are the Mahāyāna Suttas and the Chinese commentaries on them.

14 Buddhism in Japan

Prince Shōtoku

He ruled from 593 until 621 CE. Buddhism arrived in Japan from Korea in the mid-sixth century. By the time of Shōtoku's reign it had many adherents. Prince Shōtoku pronounced Buddhism the state religion. The basic text of Japanese Buddhism is the Lotus Sutta.

Amida

The Pure Land Cult of Amida, or Amitābha, was introduced from China in the eighth century. It experienced a period of rapid growth in the early thirteenth century due to the activities of reformers, the most important of whom was Honen. The cult of Amida became virtually a Japanese religion, and had great popular appeal. The Pure Land sect took the name Jodo in Japan.

Tendai

The Japanese form of T'ien t'ai. Tendai was introduced from China in the ninth century CE by Saicho, a monk who was later given the title of Dengyo Daishi – 'The Propagator of the True Religion'.

Shingon

Shingon is the Japanese form of Chen-yen. The sect was founded in Japan by Kobo (774–835), and made a significant contribution to artistic life.

Shinran (1173–1262)

He was a disciple of Honen, and was the founder of Jodoshinshu ('True Pure Land Sect'). He abandoned monasticism, married, and lived as a householder on the grounds that this was more in accord with the doctrine of reliance on Amida's grace.

Nichiren (1222–1283)

He founded a sect which was originally a reform of the Tendai sect. It became fiercely nationalistic, and was especially popular during the violent periods of the fifteenth and sixteenth centuries when Japan was engaged in a number of wars. In some respects the sect fed upon the same roots as the national – and nationalistic – religion of Shinto (Shin — heavenly beings: Tao—way). Nichiren appealed to some of Japan's military classes, but its later developments had only tenuous connections with the original teaching of Buddhism.

Zen

The Japanese name for the Ch'an form of Buddhism introduced into Japan via Korea. Zen emphasizes instantaneous enlightenment gained by meditation or by reflection upon paradoxical sayings, or koans. Zen has encouraged people to relate Buddhist insights to everyday life. It has had considerable influence in Japan on painting and poetry and has been expressed through such carefully cultivated forms as the tea ceremony. It is a form of Buddhism which has become popular in the West.

Sōtō

The Chinese form of Tsao-tung was founded by Tsao Shan and his teacher Tung Shan. It was taken to Japan by Dōgen, who established the Sōtō sect there in 1227. Sōtō uses the method of Zāzen rather than koans, and has a five-stage method of spiritual training, leading to a sense of oneness with all things.

Zāzen

A method in Zen which emphasizes meditation, and teaches the appropriate postures and breathing (rather like Yoga) to accompany meditation.

Dōgen (1200–1253)

He was the founder of the Sōtō Zen school in Japan. The best-known of his writings is 'The Eye of the True Law'. Dōgen spent the years between 1223 and 1227 in China, where he is said to have attained enlightenment. On his return to Japan he founded a Zen monastery, to which he attracted many disciples and where he developed the practice of Zāzen. Dōgen is regarded as the greatest figure in Japanese Buddhism, and in Japan he is generally looked upon as a Bodhisattva.

Rinzai

The original Rinzai sect was founded by Rinzai Gigen, also known as Lin-Chi (d.867). Rinzai was introduced into Japan by Eisai (1141–1215), and there became one of the two great sects of Zen (the other being Sōtō). The sect teaches that inspiration comes through a sudden flash of insight which can be encouraged by the use of sharp blows or sudden noises. The modern Rinzai school in Japan was founded by Hakuin Ekaku (1685–1768).

Koan

A phrase given by a master to his pupil as an exercise for the mind and a subject for meditation. The koan is sometimes in the form of a question and answer and is sometimes a simple phrase. But in either case the koan is apparently nonsensical. It is said that when the pupil sees the meaning behind the koan, then he suddenly becomes enlightened.

Examples of koans are: Question: 'Who is Buddha?' Answer: 'Three measures of flax'. Or: 'What is the sound of one hand clapping?'

Satori

Illumination or enlightenment. The word is used to describe the Buddha mind.

Sumi

Painting, used in Zen to cultivate meditation and encourage satori. Brush strokes are used economically, and many blank spaces are left to be filled in by the mind.

Haiku

Poetry in the Zen tradition which endeavours to lead the mind towards quietness. The aim of haiku is to enhance perception.

Padma-Sambhava

A well-known teacher of Tantric Buddhism who was invited to Tibet to introduce Buddhism there in the mid-eighth century CE. The form of Buddhism he took to Tibet was the Vajrayāna.

Vajrayāna

A form of Tantric Buddhism, which employed yogic practices allied to the use of magical and mystical devices, including mandalas. Tibetan Buddhism accepted from Vajrayāna traditions of non-celibate monks and magical rituals.

Mandala

A symbolic diagram usually surrounded by a circle, and often including other circles, squares, and triangles within the outer circle. The mandala is used as a basis for meditation in some schools of Hindu and Buddhist philosophy.

Atisha (Dipankara Srījnāna) (980–1053)

A Buddhist missionary to Tibet. Palace revolts and political confusion had led to the disappearance of Buddhism from Tibet, and it was re-introduced in the early eleventh century.

Atisha took with him to Tibet the Tantric Buddhism of Bihar and Bengal. It is possible that the Buddhism of Tibet, with its popular worship, its Bodhisattvas, its prayer-flags and its rituals, is some indication of the kind of Buddhism existing in a popular form in northern and eastern India before it was extinguished by the advance of Islam.

Dalai Lama

The word 'lama' means 'superior' and is a title of respect often conferred upon priests and village headmen. The Dalai Lama (Dalai was a Mongolian word meaning 'ocean') was the religious and secular leader of Tibet. To him was applied the theory of the rebirth of Bodhisattvas, and the Dalai Lamas were believed to be re-incarnations of Avalokiteśvara. The system of choosing a Dalai Lama

from boys born within a certain time of the death of the previous
Dalai Lama originated at the end of the fifteenth century. The
fourteenth Dalai Lama fled from Tibet when the Chinese invaded
the country, and is now living in exile in India.

Bibliography

A. L. Basham, *The Wonder that was India* (1954), 3rd revised ed.,
Sidgwick & Jackson 1967, Taplinger, New York 1968

E. Conze (trs.), *Buddhist Scriptures*, Penguin 1959
—— *Buddhist Thought in India*, Allen & Unwin 1962

E. B. Cowell (ed.), *Buddhist Mahayana Texts* (Sacred Books of the
East 49), 1894, reissued Dover Publications, New York 1969

H. Dumoulin, *A History of Zen Buddhism*, Eng. trs., Faber & Faber
and Random House, Toronto 1963

S. Dutt, *Buddhist Monks and Monasteries of India*, Allen & Unwin
1962

T. Ling, *A History of Religion East and West*, Macmillan 1968
—— *The Buddha*, Penguin 1976

J. Masson, *The Noble Path of Buddhism*, Open University 1977

H. Saddhatissa, *The Buddha's Way*, Allen & Unwin 1971, Braziller,
New York 1972

Sangharakshita, *The Three Jewels*, Rider 1967

D. Howard Smith, *Chinese Religions*, Weidenfeld & Nicolson and
Holt, Reinhart & Winston, New York 1968

M. E. Spiro, *Buddhism and Society*, Allen & Unwin 1970, Harper &
Row, New York 1971

Beatrice L. Suzuki, *Mahayana Buddhism*, 3rd ed., Macmillan 1969

D. T. Suzuki, *Zen and Japanese Culture*, 2nd ed., Routledge & Kegan
Paul and Pantheon Books, New York 1959

A. P. Wolf, *Religion and Ritual in Chinese Society*, Stanford University Press 1974

E. Wood, *Zen Dictionary*, Penguin 1977

16 Post-biblical Judaism

Two great themes of biblical Judaism are the Law and the Prophets. Judaism is a religion of revelation, believing that God finds his own means of communicating with his people. God speaks through creation and through the Prophets. But God speaks with the greatest precision through the Law, which is a gift to the Jewish people to enable them to know how they may serve and please God.

History is also very important in Judaism. The Jews believe that God speaks through historical events, a belief which came to be shared by Christians and Muslims. The great events of the exodus and the exile and other historical and political fortunes of the Jewish people were seen as important parts of the process of revelation. History is believed to have a purpose. It moves towards a climax, when God will send his Messiah to usher in a reign of justice, peace, and prosperity. The material world is taken very seriously, for that is where the kingdom of God is to be established.

People in Europe and North America have become more familiar with Christian interpretations of Jewish scripture than with the Jewish original, and this is significant for relationships between Christians and Jews and their understanding or misunderstanding of each other. As early as New Testament times one can trace the efforts of Christians to assert their own interpretations of Hebrew scripture, and to maintain that they knew better than the Jews how Jewish scripture is to be interpreted.

An important example of different interpretations of common material is found in Jewish and Christian understandings of the Messiah. In Jewish expectation, the coming of the Messiah will usher in a universal reign of righteousness and peace, and the appearance of a time of such beneficence may be taken as proof of the validity of the claim that the Messiah has come. So Jews have claimed that history disproves the Christian claim that Jesus is the Messiah. Against this rejection, Christians offered their interpretation of the Messiah as one who was rejected, crucified, but then raised from the dead. Such a view involved a criticism of Judaism, for the Jews had failed to recognize the Messiah, and in rejecting the Christian claim were said to be misinterpreting their own scriptures.

Christians appropriated the Jewish scriptures to themselves and termed them the Old Testament. They gave a distinctive interpretation to those scriptures. What was good and positive in the idea of the 'chosen people' was applied to the church. What was negative (the frequent acts of disobedience) was often applied to Israel. The disobedience of the Jewish people, as Christians saw it, became a popular theme of early Christian preaching and teaching, and was used to reinforce the claim that the church replaced Israel as the chosen people. This appears to have resulted in an exaggeration of Jewish opposition to Jesus and of Jewish involvement in his death.

Some modern Jewish writers, indeed, trace the origins of European anti-Semitism back to the early church. However justified that claim may be, it would be hard to deny the fact that Christians have long accepted a caricature of Judaism based upon a selective reading of the Old Testament and the critical comments about some Jews (the Pharisees, for example) in the New Testament. The Jewishness of Jesus and his first followers has been emphasized less than it might have been.[1]

But Judaism did not ossify at the end of the biblical period. Subsequent history has been as important to Jewish self-understanding as the early chronicles of the Hebrew Bible. It is partly for this reason that what follows is all about post-biblical Judaism. Another reason is that courses on Judaism, as opposed to the Old Testament, are likely to be in need of material on the post-biblical period.

The section begins with some reference to important Jewish words during the New Testament period, a time which witnessed critical developments for the Jews.

The fall of Jerusalem in 70 CE and the banning of Jews from their holy city after another revolt in 135 CE were events which determined the future shape of Judaism. The religion no longer had a centre in the temple. Before long many Jews were ejected from their Palestinian homeland, and the long centuries of wandering had begun. An important early centre of Judaism outside Palestine was in Babylon, and during the third century this became the focal point of Jewish learning.

Later events led the Jews into Europe. In Muslim Spain they found a comparatively hospitable home, and the flowering of

---

[1]See e.g. Paul Winter, *On the Trial of Jesus* (Studia Judaica 1), de Gruyter, Berlin 1961; Rosemary Reuther, *Faith and Fratricide: the Theological Roots of Anti-Semitism*, Seabury Press 1974; S. G. F. Brandon, *The Trial of Jesus*, Batsford and Stein & Day, New York 1968; C. Klein, *Anti-Judaism in Christian Theology*, Fortress Press 1977.

intellectual activity under the Moors was enjoyed by Jews as well as Arabs. In Christian Europe the Jewish experience was often less happy. The Jews became accustomed to waves of persecution and to being exiled from lands where they had settled. They were banned from England in 1290 and only allowed to return during the Commonwealth in the seventeenth century.

A feature of Jewish life in Europe was the ghetto, where Jews were forced to live together in prescribed areas and where sometimes they had to wear distinctive clothing or badges. The persecution of Jews was common in Russia and Eastern Europe at the end of the nineteenth century, and was responsible for the waves of emigrants who made their way to the USA or Britain.

The astonishing climax of this persecution occurred in Nazi Germany during the nineteen-thirties and forties, when a deliberate policy of genocide was carried out with ruthless barbarity, and six million Jews were killed.

The post-war period has seen the establishment of the State of Israel, with its attendant and unresolved problems regarding Palestinian Arabs and Israeli relationships with her Arab neighbours. It has also seen a re-evaluation by some Christian theologians of their attitudes to the Jews and Judaism which may presage happier relations in the future.

It is a remarkable fact, however, that through all the vicissitudes of its history Judaism has remained a living faith, exhibiting at times deep scholarship, profound philosophy, and firm ethical convictions. The family has always been a vital unit in the maintenance of Jewish values and religious life.

Torah

A basic word throughout the history of Judaism, Torah is the Hebrew word for the Pentateuch, the five books of the Law traditionally ascribed to Moses (although most modern scholars regard them as a collection of writings and ordinances gathered together over a long period). Torah is often translated 'law', but 'instruction' or 'teaching' renders the meaning of the word more accurately. The Torah is regarded as revelation; in the Torah God has revealed what he requires his people to do. 'Torah' is sometimes used for the entire Hebrew scriptures.

Covenant

Another vital element in the Jewish understanding of religion is the notion of an agreement between God and the people of Israel. The covenant asserts that God chose the Jewish people to be his servants and witnesses. On their side the Jews undertook to obey God by keeping the Law and so living as God's people. The other side of the agreement was seen as God's assurance that he would protect and guide his people Israel.

Sadducees

An important party among the Jews in the first century BC and the first century CE. The name is possibly derived from that of the high priest Zadok, one of David's priests. The Sadducees were drawn especially from the priestly aristocracy. In religious matters they were conservative in that they recognized only the Law of Moses (the Torah) and not the oral law. Because they refused to acknowledge development after the time of the Pentateuch, they did not accept belief in a resurrection or in angels.

A major aim of the Sadducees was the preservation of the Jewish state, and it was to this end that they collaborated with the Romans during the first century CE. The party of the Sadducees disintegrated with the fall of Jerusalem in 70 CE.

Pharisees

The Pharisees arose at the same time as the Sadducees. Their name means the 'separated ones'. They were pious people, zealous for Jewish religion and anxious not to adulterate their faith by compromising with the ruling powers, whether Syrian or Roman. In addition to the Torah, the Pharisees accepted the oral law. This was an elaboration and application of the written Law, and was justified by a tradition which held that when the Law was revealed to Moses at Sinai a series of oral instructions were also given to him, and then passed down by word of mouth.

The beliefs of the Pharisees were not restricted to what was contained in the Pentateuch and they believed, for example, in the resurrection of the dead. They were largely responsible for the survival of the faith outside Jerusalem after 70 CE, and for the early developments of rabbinic Judaism. The two great teachers among the Pharisees in the first century CE were Hillel and Shammai.

Sanhedrin

The word could be used for any council of the Jews, but normally refers to the supreme council of seventy members which met in Jerusalem during the Second Commonwealth, and was responsible for religious legislation and, within certain limits, for the administration of justice among the Jews. The Sanhedrin ceased to function in 70 CE, but an academic Sanhedrin was reconstituted in Jabneh after the fall of Jerusalem. This Sanhedrin continued in various places and with some interruptions until 425 CE.

Essenes

Jews who retired to the Dead Sea area to live a monastic life during the first century BC and the first century CE. They shunned city life and contemporary politics, and lived in great simplicity, awaiting the coming of the Messiah. The remains of one group of Essenes were discovered at Qumran when the Dead Sea Scrolls were found.

Zealots

A group of Jews in New Testament times who advocated militant resistance to the Romans. The Zealots, founded by Judas of Galilee in 6 CE, refused tribute to Rome. They were instrumental in the revolt of 66 CE which led to the Roman attack and the fall of Jerusalem in 70 CE. The Zealots continued their resistance, and 960 of them held out in the fortress at Masada until 73 CE. The Zealots had been opposed by the Sadducees, who had feared upsetting the delicate balance of their influence with Rome.

Second Hebrew Commonwealth

The period from 143 BC, when Simon Maccabaeus finally expelled the Syrians from Jerusalem, until Jerusalem fell to the Roman armies in 70 CE.

Jabneh

A town where a centre of Jewish life was re-established by the Pharisees after the fall of Jerusalem in 70 CE. A new Sanhedrin was established here, and it was at Jabneh that the canon of Jewish scripture was finalized. A leading figure in the development of Jabneh as a centre of Jewish life and learning was Rabbi Jochanan ben Zakkai.

Midrash

A method of teaching the oral Torah by the exposition of biblical texts. First used in the time of Ezra, the method of the Midrash was developed by the rabbis in the period of the re-establishment of Judaism after the fall of Jerusalem. The midrashic method can be detected in the construction of many New Testament passages.

Midrash Halachah

An exposition of Torah which resulted in a legal ruling. The word Halachah means 'walking', and the expression is derived from Ex. 18.20: 'You shall teach them the statutes and the decisions, and make them know the way in which they must walk.'

Midrash Aggadah

An exposition which is confined to moral or devotional teaching, mostly derived from the non-legal or narrative parts of scripture.

Aquila

A Greek-speaking proselyte who translated the Hebrew scriptures into Greek for the use of the many proselytes in the Roman Empire. Some quotations from Aquila's translation are found in Origen's Hexapla Bible (c. 240 CE).

Simeon bar Kochba

The leader of the Jewish revolt against the Romans in 132 CE. Some of his followers regarded him as the Messiah. Bar Kochba led the revolt for three years, until the Jews were overwhelmed by Roman armies in 135 CE.

Hadrian

Roman Emperor from 117 until 138 CE. He was responsible for the erection of a temple to Jupiter on the site of the Jerusalem temple. This act, calculated to achieve cultural and religious uniformity, led to a revolt among the Jews in 132.

Severus

A Roman general recalled from Britain by Hadrian to lead the assault on the Jewish rebels. He defeated the Jews and re-established Roman supremacy.

Aelia Capitolina

The name given to Jerusalem by the Romans after 135. The city was deliberately made into a completely non-Jewish one, and Jews were forbidden to enter on pain of death. Hadrian also closed the academic Sanhedrin at Jabneh, and issued an order forbidding the study of the Torah. Many Jews became martyrs for their faith. It was at this time that a doctrine was formulated which decreed that in order to save his life a Jew might break any of the commandments except those forbidding murder, idolatry, or incest.

9th of Ab

The anniversary of the destruction of the temple in 70 CE, and the one day during the year when Jews were allowed into Aelia Capitolina to pray at the 'Wailing Wall'.

Antoninus Pius

Hadrian's successor, and less rigorously opposed to Judaism than

Hadrian had been. During his reign (138-61 CE) a new academic Sanhedrin appeared in Galilee, at Usha.

Rabbi Simeon ben Gamaliel II
President of the Sanhedrin at Usha, and recognized by Antoninus Pius as leader of the Jewish people.

Judah the Prince (Judah ha-Nasi)
The son of and successor to Gamaliel III. Judah was instrumental in completing the Mishnah, and played an important part in the re-establishment of Palestinian Judaism after the disaster of 135.

Abba Arika
A great Jewish teacher in Babylon, who lived from 175 until 247 CE. He attracted thousands of pupils, and became known simply as 'Rab' – 'the teacher'. During the third century Palestine gradually gave way to Babylon as the centre of Judaism.

Sura
A school which arose under the influence of Abba Arika. The basis of Sura was Arika's teaching of the Mishnah of Rabbi Judah.

Judah ben Ezekiel
Another follower of Judah the Prince, who founded a rival school to that of Abba Arika at Pumbeditha.

Mishnah
The word is from a root meaning 'instruction'. The Mishnah came into existence around 200 CE, and is an authoritative collection of Jewish law and ethics. It formed the basis of the Palestinian and Babylonian Talmud. The Mishnah is said to have been compiled by Rabbi Judah (ha-Nasi).

Sedarim
Six divisions, or orders, in the Mishnah:
1. **Zera'im** Seeds. Regulations concerning agriculture.
2. **Mo'ed** Festivals. Twelve treatises, beginning with one on work prohibited on the sabbath.
3. **Nashim** Women. Seven articles on marriage and divorce.
4. **Nezikin** Damages. Ten treatises on civil laws.
5. **Kodashim** Sacred things. Eleven treatises on sacrifices that were offered in the Jerusalem temple.
6. **Tohoroth** Cleanness. Twelve articles on ritual cleanliness.

Massektoth
Sixty-three tractates, or divisions, of the Sedarim.

Perakim
Chapters within the Massektoth.

Pirke Aboth
The 'Chapters (i.e. Sayings) of the Fathers', included in the Nezikin.

Baraitha
'External' teachings. These were the teachings of other rabbis which were separate from the Mishnah of Rabbi Judah.

Tosefta
'Additional' teachings, added by other rabbis. Baraitha and Tosefta contributed to the formulation of new legal judgments, and included rival traditions and teachings to those found in the Mishnah.

Halachoth
New legal judgments, based upon the Mishnah together with the additions of Baraitha and Tosefta.

Gemara
The word means 'completion', and refers to the completed version of the Mishnah together with the various additions made by other rabbis.

Tannaim
Specialists in the teaching of the Mishnah.

Talmud
From a root meaning 'to study'. The Talmud is made up of the Mishnah and the Gemara. There are two versions, the Babylonian and the Palestinian. The Babylonian Talmud was the product of the schools of Abba Arika and others, and developed in circumstances that were congenial for study. The Palestinian Talmud was a more hurried piece of work. It was completed in the middle of the fourth century, when conditions were difficult for Jews living under Christian influence in Palestine.

Maaseh Bereshith
Writing related to the Talmud and referring, as the name implies, to the work of creation. It is a mystical speculation based upon the first chapter of Genesis.

Maaseh Merkabah

The Maaseh Merkabah (which is referred to in the Mishnah as well as the Talmud) contains an exposition of Ezekiel's vision of the divine chariot. The Merkabah was regarded as a secret doctrine, to be transmitted only to the worthy.

Midrash Rabbah

Homiletical material, covering the Pentateuch, Canticles, Ruth, Lamentations, Ecclesiastes and Esther.

Tanchuma Midrashim

A collection of homiletical material made by Tanchuma ben Abba, a famous Palestinian Aggadist of the fourth century.

Targum

An Aramaic translation, or paraphrase, of Jewish scripture.

Rabina

The last leader of the Sura, in Babylonia. The development of the Talmud, by the addition of homiletical material, came to an end with the death of Rabina, in 500 CE. The Babylonian Talmudic tradition states that Rab Ashi (d. 427) and Rabina were the last of the teachers.

Theodosius II

The emperor under whom the Jewish Patriarchate in Palestine was finally abolished in 425. This action was followed by the closure of the academic Sanhedrin.

17 Jewish belief

Shema

Literally 'hear', from Deut. 6.4–5, 'Hear, O Israel: the Lord our God is one Lord; and you shall love the Lord your God with all your heart, and with all your soul, and with all your might.' This is a basic affirmation of faith, recited daily by devout Jews. The Shema emphasizes the firm Jewish belief in monotheism.

Elohim

The Hebrew plural of the word 'god'. In Hebrew 'El', the singular form, is sometimes used to refer to the 'gods' of surrounding nations at the time when the Jews settled in Palestine. When referring to the one God, the plural form of Elohim was used within a certain Pentateuchal tradition.

Yahweh

The Hebrew letters YHWH appear in the scriptures as a name for God. But since the Hebrew script did not include the vowel sounds there is some doubt about how the word should be pronounced, although most scholars now agree that 'Yahweh' is the most likely rendering. The difficulty is compounded by the fact that from the time of the Babylonian exile the Hebrews refused to pronounce the 'name' of God and so would say 'Adonai' (=Lord) whenever YHWH appeared in the text. (The form 'Jehovah' arose much later when Christian scholars mistakenly combined the vowels of Adonai with the consonants of YHWH.)

Hefqer

The word means 'ownerless', and is used with the negative as a description of the world. The doctrine of creation and of God's continuing concern for the world implies that the world is not hefqer.

Ha-Geburah

'The might', a Talmudic phrase used to express God's omnipotence.

Shechinah (Shekinah)

'The indwelling', a Talmudic phrase which expresses God's omnipresence, and suggests that God is immanent within the world as well as transcendent. The idea is not the same as pantheism, although it does suggest that there is no place without God.

Shuttaf

'Partner', a word which expresses man's role as God's partner in the creative process.

Kingdom of God

An important element in Jewish belief is the idea that the kingdom of God will one day be established on earth, bringing a reign of universal justice, peace, goodness and truth. The primary meaning of the kingdom of God is within the present world, but after the development of Jewish apocalyptic the expression has also come to have a supra-historical and supernatural meaning.

Onaath Debarim

'Wrongdoing in words', an offence of deceit which is considered to be more grave than a practical offence.

Onaath Mamon

Wrongdoing in material affairs.

Genebath Daath

'Stealing the mind' of another person by misrepresentation.

Zedakah

Righteousness, a concept which includes the idea that God is the true owner of the world and all that is in it. Man holds goods in trust for God, and so misuse of material goods in order to exploit or oppress others is an offence against God. Zedakah also includes the practice of charity; the indigent person has a right to help from those who are blessed with possessions.

Gemiluth Chasadim

The practice of good deeds, including courtesy towards others, visiting the sick, and encouraging other people in good conduct. This relates to the need to express love in human relationships, as enjoined in the commandment to 'love the alien as a man like yourself' (Lev. 19.34).

Holiness

The basic notion of holiness is of separation. God is holy because he is totally other than man. People are holy in so far as they belong to God. Personal holiness is enjoined upon the Jew: 'You shall be holy because I, the Lord your God, am holy' (Lev. 19.2).

Kiddush ha-Shem

The sanctification of God's name. All that brings credit on Israel, her religion and her people, through service and self-sacrifice, sanctifies God's name. The highest expression of this is in martyrdom.

Ghillul ha-Shem

The tarnishing of the name of God through bad conduct.

Philo (c. 20/25 BC–40/50 CE)
An Alexandrian Jew, and one of the great philosophers of Judaism. He attempted to reconcile Jewish theology, based upon the scriptures, with Greek philosophy, and in so doing he adopted an allegorical interpretation of scripture. He developed the notion of the logos as an intermediary between God and the world. His hellenizing of Jewish thought had an influence upon early Christianity, and especially upon the Christians of Alexandria.

Rabbi Saadiah ben Joseph al-Fayyumi (Saadiah, or Saadya) (892–942)
The first in the line of the great Jewish medieval philosophers. Saadiah regarded reason as an important means of arriving at religious truth, and taught that revelation and reason are a unity. Born in Egypt, he was influenced by the Muslim Kalamists, and his writing shows the influence of both Greek and Arabic philosophy. His major work, *The Book of Beliefs and Opinions*, written in Arabic, was the first great book of Jewish rationalist thought since the time of Philo.

Solomon ibn Gabirol
The first great Jewish philosopher of Moorish Spain, and also a poet. Solomon, who lived in the first half of the eleventh century, wrote in Arabic, and was the author of *Mekor Hayyim* ('Fountain of Life'). Spain under Muslim rule was an area in which Judaism was able to flourish.

Kether Malehuth
'Royal Crown', a poem by Gabirol which is read in many congregations on the Day of Atonement.

Judah Halevi (1085–1140)
Jewish philosopher, born in Toledo, in Spain. He was the author of *Kuzari* – 'A Book in Defence of the Despised and Humiliated Faith', in which he attempted to show the superiority of Judaism over Islam

and Christianity. Written in the form of a dialogue, *Kuzari* distinguishes carefully between revelation and reason, 'the God of Abraham' and 'the God of Aristotle', and warns Jews against the danger of being misled by Greek philosophy. Judah Halevi also emphasized the covenant and the divine election of Israel.

Abraham ibn Daud

A rabbi and a rationalist, he was concerned to reconcile Jewish faith and philosophy. There is, he taught, no conflict between faith and the philosophy of Aristotle, although what Gentiles groped after has been revealed to Israel. He accepted the philosophical concept of God as the Prime Mover. He was the author of *Emunah Ramah*, or 'Exalted Faith', which he wrote c. 1180.

Moses Maimonides (1134/35-1204)

Regarded as the greatest philosopher of Spanish Jewry, Maimonides was strongly Aristotelian in outlook and adopted a rationalistic attitude towards, for example, the Decalogue and miracles. Maimonides formulated the thirteen articles of faith which have since been regarded as the essential beliefs of Judaism. These included 'Belief that Moses was the greatest of all prophets' (contra Islam), and 'Belief in the coming of the Messiah' (contra Christianity).

Levi ben Gerson (1288-1334)

He argued against much of the work of Maimonides in a book called *Melchamoth Hashem*, 'Battle for the Name'.

Hisdai Crescas (1340-1410)

Also a strong critic of Maimonides, he tried to free Judaism from the influence of Aristotle. His arguments against Aristotle were used by Pico della Mirandola and Giordano Bruno. By the time of Crescas the Jewish centre of influence had shifted to Christian Spain, where Hebrew as well as Arabic translations of Aristotle were available.

Sefer ha-Ikkarim

'The Book of Fundamental Principles', written by Joseph Albo, a disciple of Crescas. This aimed at defending Judaism against Christianity, which had by this time become the main opponent of Judaism in Spain.

Kabbalah

The name means 'tradition', and refers to an esoteric tradition which is part of Jewish mysticism. It developed in Spain and southern France in the thirteenth century, although it drew upon traditions based on the Maaseh Bereshith and the Maaseh Merkabah (see pp. 88 f.). The Kabbalists drew a distinction between the transcendent God, about whom nothing can be predicated, and the God who is encountered in religious experience. To the transcendent God the Kabbalists gave the name En Sof, the Infinite. The transcendent God makes himself known by a process of emanation.

Kabbalist teaching included the idea that the unity and perfection of God depends upon the union of male and female principles, and so it incorporated into its mysticism a reinforcement of the importance of the married state and of sex for human perfection.

Sefiroth

The ten aspects of manifestation through which God reveals himself. According to Kabbalah the most important are the sixth sefira, Tif'ereth, which is conceived of as a dynamic force and described in symbolism of male power as the King and the Bridegroom, and the tenth sefira, Shechinah or Malkuth, the aspect of the divine which is regarded as being closest to the material world, and is described by female symbols of the Bride and the Queen.

Zohar

The word means 'splendour'. The Zohar is a form of a commentary on the Pentateuch, written partly in Aramaic and partly in Hebrew. It is said to have been compiled from various sources by Moses de Leon (d. 1305), but is ascribed by some to Simeon ben Yochai, who lived in the second century CE. The Zohar uses four methods of scriptural interpretation,: Peshat, or literal interpretation; Remez, or allegory; Derush, or exposition; Sod, or mystical interpretation.

19 Jewish practice

Rabbi

A leader of Jewish congregations. The rabbi is not ordained as a priest. He is normally a learned man, especially in matters relating to the Torah. The rabbi normally reads the lessons and gives the addresses in the synagogue. In many Western countries he is a full-time official and fulfils a role very similar to that of priests and ministers in Christian churches.

Synagogue

A Jewish meeting-place for worship, also known as Beth ha-Kenesset, or House of Assembly. In the early history of Israel the Jerusalem temple was regarded as essential for true worship. The beginnings of the synagogue can be traced back to the time of the Babylonian exile, in the sixth century BC, when Jews who were separated from the temple had to devise alternative means of worship. The synagogue was in common use in Palestine by the first century BC, and after the fall of Jerusalem it became the normal place of worship.

The synagogue service consists of prayers, readings from the Torah and the Prophets, and a sermon. In Reform synagogues hymns are also used. In Orthodox synagogues the service is mostly in Hebrew, whilst in Liberal and Reform congregations the vernacular is more commonly used. Synagogues are built to face towards Jerusalem.

Tallith

The tallith is a fringed garment worn as a scarf or prayer shawl during the synagogue service. It has embroidered corners from each of which is suspended a tzitzith, a cord of eight threads and with five knots.

Tefillin

Small containers, also known as phylacteries, which are attached by a cord to the head or arm. They contain a scriptural text.

Mezuzah

A small container attached to the doorpost, and containing a text. The Mezuzah and Tefillin comply with the injunction contained in Deut. 6.8-9, referring to the commandments: 'Bind them as a sign on the hand and wear them as a phylactery on the forehead; write them up on the doorposts of your houses and on your gates.'

Tefillah

Meaning 'prayer', the word refers to the principal part of each of the three daily prayers, popularly known as Amidah ('standing').

Kashrut

The dietary laws of Judaism, which forbid the eating of meat from any animal which is not slaughtered in the prescribed Jewish manner and any animal that does not both chew the cud and divide the hoof. Also forbidden are fish that do not have both scales and fins, and the taking of milk or milk-products after meat.

Kosher
Food which accords with the dietary laws.

Sabbath
The last day of the week, observed as a day of rest (cf. Gen. 2.1–3; Ex. 20.8–11). Great importance is attached to the observance of the sabbath in Judaism. Sabbath begins at sunset on Friday and continues until sunset on Saturday. The three main elements in the observance of the sabbath are: rest from work and ordinary weekly activities, the celebration and worship of a family festival, and synagogue services. The Sabbath begins in a Jewish home with the recitation of the Kiddush, a prayer of thanksgiving for the gift of the sabbath.

Bar-Mitzvah
A ceremony to mark the achievement of religious maturity on the part of a Jewish boy, at the age of thirteen. The ceremony includes the reading of a passage of the Torah in Hebrew by the boy. After that he is regarded as a full member of the synagogue. An equivalent ceremony for girls has been introduced in recent times, although it does not have the full solemnity and significance of Bar-Mitzvah.

Rosh Hashanah
The Jewish New Year, which occurs on the first day of Tishri (September/October). It is celebrated as the anniversary of creation, with the idea that on that day people should give account to God for the world comitted to their care. Rosh Hashanah is followed by ten days of repentance which culminate in Yom Kippur.

Shofar
A ram's horn, blown in places of worship on Rosh Hashanah as a call to repentance and a reminder that God is the king of the universe.

Yom Kippur
The Day of Atonement, the most solemn day in the Jewish year, celebrated on the tenth day of Tishri. The day is marked by lengthy synagogue services which have an emphasis on confession.

Passover (Pesach)
A festival which recalls the exodus from Egypt, celebrated on the

fourteenth day of Nisan (March/April). It is an eight-day festival, during which only unleavened bread is eaten in memory of the flight from Egypt. Passover is also a spring festival.

Seder

The word means 'order', and refers to the order of the ritual of the Passover meal. The meal includes unleavened bread and bitter herbs to commemorate the hasty departure from Egypt and the bitterness of the wilderness wanderings.

Shavuoth (Pentecost)

The Feast of Weeks. A festival of the wheat harvest, which is also associated with the giving of the ten commandments. It is celebrated fifty days after Passover.

Sukkoth (Booths, or Tabernacles)

A seven-day festival which marked the end of the harvest season in the early Palestinian agricultural cycle. It was a time when people moved out into the fields and the vineyards, living in tents, while the final work in the fields was done before the winter rain. Celebrated on the fifteenth Tishri, the festival is a time of thanksgiving for gifts. It also commemorates the forty years of wandering in the wilderness. The two days following the festival are devoted to the adoration of the Law and the study of the Torah.

Purim

A festival which celebrates the story of Esther, the Jewess who became queen of the Persian King Xerxes, and then courageously helped her fellow Jews by thwarting the anti-Jewish plot of Xerxes' vizier, Haman. Purim is a popular and joyful festival, accompanied by the giving and receiving of gifts.

Chanukkah (Hanukkah)

A festival celebrating the victory of Judas Maccabaeus over Antiochus Epiphanes of Syria in 165 BC. Chanukkah falls close to Christmas, and is also in some ways a festival of light. A feature of the festival is the lighting of lamps; one candle of the eight-branched candelabra is lit on each of the eight days of the festival.

9th of Ab

A fast commemorating the destruction of the temple. A rabbinic tradition held that the first and second temples were both destroyed on the ninth day of Ab (in 586 BC and 70 CE). A solemn period of nine days precedes the fast, which occurs in July/August (see p. 86).

Yom Haatzmaut
The Day of Independence of Israel, which falls in April/May, and is celebrated as the anniversary of the birth of the Jewish State.

Chuppah
The canopy under which the marriage ceremony is conducted. Normally this is erected within the synagogue.

---

20 Modern Judaism

Ashkenazim
One of the main groups of Jews (the other being the Sephardim). There are differences between the two in a number of matters, including the application of the Law, liturgy, and the pronunciation of Hebrew. Some Jewish scholars trace the differences between the two groups well back into Jewish history. But the actual identity of the groups emerged during the Middle Ages, when there was a distinction between the Jews of France and Germany (and later of Poland and other parts of Eastern Europe) and the Jews of the Iberian peninsula. The Ashkenazim were the Jews of Central and Eastern Europe, who spoke Yiddish. Their rabbis concentrated their scholarly efforts on the study of the Talmud because of the difficulties Jews had in sharing in the wider culture of Christian Europe.

Sephardim
The Jews of Spain and Portugal, who lived for centuries under Muslim rule and were able to share in the progress of learning among the Moors. They were expelled from the Iberian Peninsula between 1492 and 1498 (when the area was once again under Christian domination), but their descendants are still known as Sephardim.

The Sephardim were linked with the traditions of Babylonian Jewry, whereas the Ashkenazim reflected the influence of Judaism in Palestine.

Rabbi Israel ben Eliezer (Ba'al Shem Tov) (1700–1760)

A Polish Jew who was the founder of a new Polish mystical sect which rejected asceticism and emphasized the joy of worship. In the movement which gathered around him there was the beginning of modern Hasidism. He was known as the Ba'al Shem Tov, 'the Master of the Good Name.'

Hasidism

There were people known as Hasidim (or Chasidim), the pious ones, iɴ Maccabaean times. They were Jews who stressed purely religious values and took no part in the fighting against the Syrians. The eighteenth-century group of Hasidim, however, had no direct connection with the earlier one. They were a group of Eastern European Jewish mystics who arose out of the teaching of Rabbi Israel ben Eliezer. They encouraged ecstatic prayer and worship in a reaction against the Talmudic teaching of the time. The Hasidim also showed tendencies towards pantheism.

Moses Mendelssohn (1729–1786)

A prominent German Jewish philosopher who sought an accommodation with European Christian society. He regarded reason as the basis of Judaism. Mendelssohn taught that there are three articles of faith: belief in the existence of God, the immortality of the soul, and divine Providence. These he deemed to be shared by all true religions. The particular contribution of Judaism, he thought, lay in law rather than in revelation. Many Jews who were influenced by Mendelssohn regarded his teaching as an encouragement to conversion to Christianity.

David Friedlander (1756–1834)

Friedlander was a follower of Mendelssohn, and the founder of Reform Judaism. He aimed to establish a form of Judaism less obviously foreign to a European environment, and so encouraged the use of German (and later of other vernaculars) in place of Hebrew in the synagogue service.

Israel Jacobson (1768–1828)

A contemporary of Friedlander, Jacobson founded the first Jewish Reform Temple in 1810, and introduced German prayers, a sermon, and the use of the organ into the worship.

Reform Judaism

Later leaders of Reform Judaism in Germany promoted the idea that

Judaism is entirely a religious affair and not at all a national one. Synagogue services became closer to church services in their form. Men and women sat together. There was even a suggestion that the day of worship should be changed from Saturday to Sunday, although this was rejected. The centre of Reform Judaism later moved to the USA.

Samson Raphael Hirsch (1808–1888)

An opponent of Reform Judaism, Hirsch reasserted the values of traditional Judaism. He is regarded as the founder of neo-Orthodoxy in Judaism. This movement attempted to regain the insights and values of Judaism during the Spanish/Arabic period.

Zionism

The term was coined in the eighteen-nineties to describe a movement for the establishment of an autonomous Jewish community in Palestine. The Choveve Zion movement was founded at a conference in Kattowitz, Russia, in 1884, whilst the first Zionist Congress was convened by Theodore Herzl at Basel in 1897. In 1895 Herzl had published a book, *Judenstaat*, which advocated a Jewish home in Palestine. These activities led to the establishment of Jewish villages and agricultural settlements in Palestine.

Zionism claimed most of its support from Orthodox Jews. The majority of Reform Jews were opposed to the movement in its earlier years. An important stage in the Zionist struggle was marked by the Balfour Declaration of the British Government in 1917, which included the words: 'HM Government view with favour the establishment in Palestine of a national home for the Jewish people'. However, it was not until after the Second World War and much fighting in Palestine that the State of Israel was founded on 14 May 1948.

Holocaust

A word used to describe the deliberate extermination of Jewish people by Nazi Germany in the nineteen-thirties and forties. During that period six million Jews, or one third of the total world Jewish population, were killed.

Bibliography

H. H. Ben-Sasson, *A History of the Jewish People*, Harvard University Press and Weidenfeld & Nicolson 1976

Philip Birnbaum, *A Book of Jewish Concepts*, Hebrew Publishing Co., New York 1964

Encyclopaedia Judaica, Jerusalem 1971–72

Isidore Epstein, *Judaism*, Penguin 1959

David Goldstein, *The Religion of the Jews*, Open University 1978

H. J. Zimmels, *Ashkenazim and Sephardim*, Oxford University Press 1958

21 Islam

Islam began with the life and work of the prophet Muhammad in the seventh century of the Christian Era. Muhammad proclaimed to the tribespeople of Arabia a religion which emphasized the uniqueness and transcendence of God and the need to submit completely to his will. After some initial conflicts Islam achieved astonishing success, and spread widely and rapidly. It replaced the polytheistic religion of the Arabs, and then extended around the Mediterranean coast. Within 120 years of the death of Muhammad Islam had spread along the North African coast and into Spain, whilst in the East it had extended through Afghanistan and reached as far as the river Indus. In the early period of growth, under the Umayyad dynasty, the political centre of Islam was in Damascus and the desert Arabs were the dominant Muslim people. In 762, under the 'Abbāsids, the centre shifted to Baghdad, and Persian influence became increasingly important. Other great centres of Islam were Cairo, where the Fātimid dynasty was established, Cordova, after the conquest of Spain by the Muslims, and Istanbul, after its capture by the Turks. The early and rapid spread of Islam, in which process other religions were supplanted, reinforced the Muslim understanding of history which regarded success as justification of the truth of Islamic faith.

Islam places great emphasis upon the duty of man to obey God. Allāh is too far beyond the grasp of human minds or imaginations for him to be known by any human process. Allāh reveals himself through the prophet Muhammad and the Qur'ān. The appropriate response for man is to obey Allāh by following the clear duties laid upon every Muslim. The 'Five Pillars' of Islam define these duties. The Qur'ān in Arabic is regarded by orthodox Muslims as the infallible word of God, and the belief in divine revelation involved in this notion is an important part of Islamic faith. The message of Allāh, given through his prophet Muhammad and recorded in the Qur'ān is believed to be the final revelation, displacing or fulfilling the earlier revelations given to the Jews and to the Christians.

In the West the rise of Islam had important repercussions for

Christendom. For the first time for many centuries Christianity was faced by a faith which challenged its own; a faith, moreover, which established a presence in Europe. There were many things that Europe learned from Islam, including important aspects of science and mathematics which were transmitted from India and the East via the Arab world. Arabic influence worked upon Europe and played some part in the rise of the Renaissance. But Christian Europe also found itself faced by a formidable military foe, and the unfortunate episode of the Crusades was one expression of European frustration with its powerful neighbour. And in its early growth Islam displaced some of the most important centres of early Christianity.

Islam also had a strong influence on the history of India. Muslim invaders began systematically to raid the plains of India in the tenth century, following upon the earlier success of Arab conquerors of the Sind in the eighth century CE. They gradually penetrated further eastwards. By the end of the twelfth century the Muslims had reached the east coast and controlled almost the whole of North India.

In the sixteenth century the Mughals entered India and established the dynasty which was finally extinguished only after the Indian Mutiny, in 1858. The Mughals established a strongly centralized and efficiently-administered empire, and they left their architecture and art as lasting memorials of their presence in India.

Today Islam is a world faith. Whilst still dominant in the Middle East, Islam is also the main religion of Pakistan, Malaysia, and Indonesia, and most Muslims in today's world live to the east and south of Karachi. There are also many Muslims in Europe. It is difficult to obtain precise information about numbers, but it is probable that there are between one and two million Muslims in Britain today. The building of new mosques and the increasing importance of the Arab economy to the West both indicate the significance of Islam for the Western world.

Islam

The Faith. The word is derived from roots which mean submission or peace. Islam indicates the basic conviction of Muslims that truth is revealed by an omnipotent God. Man's proper response to what is revealed to him is to submit. When he does so his life will be properly ordered. Muslims hold that islam can be seen in the true submission of man to God in any age, including pre-Islamic times, and in any religious system, although Islam is usually written with a capital, and refers to the religion, society, and culture of the Muslim.

Muslim

The believer. One who makes the submission of Islam. (The terms

'Muhammadan' and 'Muhammadanism' should be avoided since they may give the impression, offensive to Muslims, that the prophet Muhammad is the object of worship). Whilst Islam is firmly rooted in the Arab lands its geographical spread is such that more than half the world's Muslims are to be found east and south of Karachi. In recent years Muslims have come as immigrants to Britain and other European countries and although no reliable statistics based upon religious observance are yet available it is probably that there are now between one and two million Muslims in Britain.

Muhammad (born 570, died 8 June 632)

The founder of Islam. He experienced a number of visions in which it is claimed that the angel Gabriel spoke to him and gave him a message to deliver to his fellow Arabs. Muhammad's message was critical of contemporary Arabic religious practice, much of which was idolatrous, and emphasized the unity and greatness of God. After some initial setbacks Muhammad achieved astonishing success in spreading his message and winning converts. By the time of his death the whole of the Arabian peninsula was under the dominance of Islam.

'Abdallah ibn 'Abd al-Muttalib

Father of Muhammad, who died a few months before the birth of the prophet. The family fulfilled duties as custodians of the shrine at Mecca.

Āminah

Mother of Muhammad. She did not long survive her son's birth, and Muhammad was orphaned at an early age.

Abū Tālib

Uncle of Muhammad, and responsible for most of the prophet's upbringing.

Khadijah

Muhammad's first wife. She was the owner of caravans trading out of Mecca and was a widow, aged forty, when she married Muhammad, who was then twenty-five. She was a great encourager of Muhammad during the period of his visions and the earlier part of his public activity.

Quraish (Quraysh)

An Arabian tribe, some of whose members acted as custodians of the Ka'bah. Muhammad's family belonged to this tribe, although when he began his career as a prophet he came into conflict with members of the Quraish, who naturally resisted the thoroughgoing reform of religion proposed by Muhammad.

'Abd Manāf

Muhammad's branch of the Quraish tribe.

Mecca

A place in Saudi Arabia, and birthplace of Muhammad. Mecca was once a great trading centre. It is now the geographical and spiritual focal point of Islam, towards which Muslims turn in prayer and to which they go on pilgrimage. Muslims associate Mecca with some of the stories of Abraham.

Ka'bah

The word means 'cube', and refers to a stark cube-shaped building within the precincts of the great mosque at Mecca. The Ka'bah, which is fifteen metres high, is normally draped with a black cloth. It houses the black stone which was a significant object of worship in pre-Islamic Arabia, and tradition associates the building of the Ka'bah with Abraham and Ishmael. The Ka'bah provides a physical focus for pilgrims to Mecca and for prayer.

Qiblah

The direction towards the Ka'bah in Mecca from any other point, indicated in a mosque by the mihrāb.

Medina

A city some 180 miles north of Mecca to which Muhammad and about a hundred of his followers went in 622 CE. Previously known as Yathrib, the city was renamed Medīnat al-Nabī, 'the city of the prophet'. Medina is the second most sacred city to Muslims, and contains the tombs of Muhammad and of the first two Caliphs.

Muhājirūn

A word meaning 'emigrants', and used to describe the followers of Muhammad who emigrated from Mecca to Medina in 622.

Hijrah

'The breaking of the ties'. The event of the migration from Mecca to Medina in 622 when it became difficult for the prophet to remain in Mecca. Muhammad arranged with pilgrims from Yathrib for his followers to go to their city, and accompanied by Abū Bakr he followed later. This move was decisive for the development of Islam, and Islamic history takes its starting point from Hijrah. The Muslim calendar begins from 622 CE, and years are denoted by the initials AH (after Hijrah). The fact that the group which migrated with Muhammad to Medina found its identity in belief rather than simply in kinship ties was of great significance, and pointed towards the unifying power of Islam in the Arab world.

Hanīf

One who did not join in idolatrous worship in pre-Islamic times. In the Qur'ān the title is used especially of Abraham.

Badr

The site of a famous battle, twenty miles south-west of Medina, at which Muhammad and 300 followers defeated over 1000 Meccans.

Uhud

A battle after Badr at which the Muslims suffered a setback. 3000 Meccans attacked Medina and were engaged in battle outside the city near the hill of Uhud. The Muslims repelled an infantry attack, but were overcome by the Meccan cavalry. But the Meccans did not follow up their success. Muslims later explained this reverse as a testing by Allāh.

Jihād

The holy war. The concept was first formulated by Muhammad during battles with the Meccans. As Islam spread, polytheists were sometimes offered a choice between accepting Islam or being put to the sword, whereas people of the Book (Jews and Christians) were able to pay a tax as a token of submission to Muslim rule whilst continuing in their own religion.

Abū Sufyān

A Meccan opponent of Muhammad who surrendered and accepted Islam in AH 3.

Khālid ibn al-Walīd

A dominant figure in the conquests of the rebellious Arab tribesmen after the death of Muhammad.

Caliph (Khalīfa)

The name means 'deputy' or 'representative', and was given to leaders of the Muslim community after the death of the prophet. The Caliphate was at first centred at Medina. The fourth Caliph, 'Alī, moved the centre to Kūfah in Iraq. From 661 to 750 CE, the period of the Umayyad dynasty, Damascus was the capital of the Caliphs. In 762, with the rise of the 'Abbāsids, the Caliphate moved to Baghdad, and in 1517 it was moved by the Turks to Istanbul. The Caliphate was finally abolished by Ataturk in 1923.

Rāshidūn

The four 'rightly guided' Caliphs: Abū Bakr, 'Umar, 'Uthmān, and 'Alī.

Abū Bakr

The father-in-law of Muhammad, and the first Caliph, who succeeded the prophet in his role as leader of the Muslim community. He was Caliph for only two years, and died in 634.

'Umar I (ibn al-Khattāb)

Caliph from 634 to 644. His leadership marked a period of great advance for Islam. By the time of his death Islam covered Iraq, Syria, Lower Egypt and parts of North Africa, and to the east had reached as far as western Persia. 'Umar was stabbed in the mosque at Medina in 644.

'Uthmān

Uncle of the prophet, 'Uthmān was Caliph from 644 until 656. This period saw the continued advance of Islam, including the building up of a fleet in the Mediterranean. It was during 'Uthmān's leadership that the final and authorized version of the Qur'ān was produced.

Sunnīs

The party of mainstream orthodoxy. They held that the Caliph should come from Muhammad's own tribe of Quraish.

'Alī (ibn Abī-Tālib)

A cousin and son-in-law of the prophet, 'Alī was Caliph from 656 until 661. He held that his descendants, the Alīds, had an exclusive right to the Caliphate. 'Alī was assassinated in 661.

Mu'āwiya ibn Abi-Sufyān

Mu'āwiya was governor of Syria. He was in open conflict with 'Alī after the death of 'Uthmān, and refused to accept 'Alī as Caliph. When 'Alī died in 661, Mu'āwiya was acknowledged as Caliph throughout the Islamic empire, with the exception of the minority movement around 'Alī. Mu'āwiya was the founder of the Umayyad Caliphate, which ruled from Damascus from 661 until 750.

Hasan

A son of 'Alī, Hasan was killed in Medina.

Husain

The other son of 'Alī, Husain was murdered by Sunnīs. His death was a crucial event in the development of Shī'ah Islam, and is remembered in the Muharram festival.

Karbalā (Kerbelā)

A place in Iraq where Husain and his followers were massacred by Sunnīs in 680.

Shī'ah

A minority movement within Islam which is to be distinguished from the Sunnī majority. The word Shī'ah means a sect. The Shī'ahs grew out of the experiences of 'Alī and his followers. The opposition which they endured led them to question the Islamic doctrine that historical and political success verifies religious truth. The Shī'ahs saw religious value in adversity and suffering. The main centres of Shī'ah Islam are in Iraq, Persia, Lebanon, Pakistan and India, and East Africa.

Imām

For Sunnī Muslims, the Imām is simply the leader of a congregation. He is likely to be regarded as a learned man, especially in knowledge of the Qur'ān, but he is not ordained. For Shī'ahs, the Imāms have had a special significance. They regard authority as residing in the Imāms as successors of the family of 'Alī rather than in Ijtihād, as Sunnīs hold it (see p. 113). Shī'ahs also hold to the idea of a hidden Imām who will be disclosed one day.

Umayyad Caliphs

The dynasty which ruled from Damascus from 661 until 750. Strongly influenced by the desert Arabs, they extended Islamic power along the North African coast and into Spain, and in the east they penetrated Afghanistan and reached as far as the river Indus. After the overthrow of the Caliphate in Damascus Umayyad rule was established in Spain, where a great centre of learning and culture was founded at Cordova.

'Abbāsid Caliphs

The 'Abbāsid Caliphate lasted from 750 until 1258. In 762 the Caliphate moved to Baghdad, where scholars translated many Greek books into Arabic, with important consequences for the promotion of philosophy, theology, and the practical sciences. During this period Persian influence became strong in the Islamic world.

Fātimid

An Egyptian dynasty, founded in Tunisia by 'Ubaydallah, who claimed descent from Fātimah, the daughter of Muhammad. The focal point of the Fātimid dynasty was Cairo, and the Egyptian city became a great centre for the Islamic world as the power of the 'Abbāsid empire and the influence of Baghdad declined. The Fātimid movement was a branch of Ismā'ilite Shī'ism.

Seljuks

Originally nomads from the Steppes of Central Asia, the Seljuks became militant Sunnīs and established a great Turkish dynasty.

Sultanate

The office of the temporal ruler, instituted by the Seljuks, who left the Caliph in control of religious affairs.

Saladin

A great Seljuk Sultan who opposed the Crusaders and in 1187 recaptured Jerusalem from the Christians.

Mongols

A warlike people from eastern Siberia who achieved great military success in the thirteenth and fourteenth centuries and expanded into China, Western Asia, Russia, Germany and Poland. In 1258 they captured Baghdad, and various branches of the western Mongols eventually adopted Islam.

Ghāzī

Originally mercenary soldiers among the Turks who lived partly on the booty they won in battle. But the Ghāzīs also had religious roots in mystical traditions of Islam, and were the more feared for the fanaticism which this inspired.

Ottoman

A Turkish empire, the origins of which are to be found in the successes of groups of Ghāzīs. In 1354 they entered Europe, subduing Serbia and Bulgaria. In the sixteenth century they conquered most of Hungary and reached almost to Vienna. They dominated the Mediterranean, and were a terror to Christian Europe on many fronts.

The Ottoman Empire declined during the seventeenth century, but only finally expired after the First World War.

---

22   Islamic belief and devotion

Qur'ān (Koran)

The scriptures of Islam, believed to have been revealed to Muhammad by the angel Gabriel in a series of visions. Written in Arabic, the Qur'ān is regarded by Muslims as the infallible word of God. The Qur'ān stresses the sovereignty of Allāh and Muhammad's role as the final prophet. It includes references to many biblical characters, including Abraham, Moses, and Jesus, and provides an Islamic explanation of these figures as true prophets whose message attains a final form in the revelation given through Muhammad.

Allāh

God, who is the Creator and supreme Ruler of the Universe, known by men only in so far as he chooses to reveal himself. The firm monotheism of Muhammad was a vital part of his message to the Arabia of his time, and the unity of God remains a major tenet of Islamic belief.

Shirk

A word which means 'association'. Muslims regard it as a great sin to associate anything or anyone with Allāh. It was partly the fear of committing shirk that discouraged Muslims from using human or even animal forms in religious art and encouraged instead the development of geometrical designs and calligraphy.

Wahy

Inspiration. A state in which personal thought is suspended and a man becomes the vehicle of divine inspiration. The Qur'ān is believed to have been transmitted to Muhammad while he was in this state.

Surah

The name given to the chapters of the Qur'ān, which is divided into

114 surahs. After the first surah the divisions are generally according to length rather than to chronology or content. The longer surahs are at the beginning and the shorter ones at the end.

Tanzīl

A divine 'sending down' of the truth, which expresses the idea that the Qur'ān was given by Allāh to a passive recipient.

I'jāz

The miraculous quality of the Qur'ān, testifying to its divine origin.

Hāfiz al-Qur'ān

Committing the Qur'ān to memory.

Dhikr

The practice of reciting short passages from the Qur'ān as a devotional act, sometimes with the aid of a rosary. Dhikr is especially practised among sūfis.

Kalimah

The declaration of faith of a Muslim: 'There is no God but Allāh, and Muhammad is his messenger.'

Bismillāh

The title given to the invocation of the divine name – 'In the name of God, the merciful, the compassionate' – with which all but one of the surahs of the Qur'ān begin. It is also used in Muslim acts of devotion.

Fātihah

'The Opener'. The first surah of the Qur'ān, and held in special reverence. The Fātihah is in the form of a prayer, and is commonly used in public and private prayer.

al-Rahmān

The merciful, a word which describes Allāh's nature as a God of mercy.

al-Rahim

The compassionate, a word which expresses the practice of mercy by Allāh.

al-Asmā al-Husnā

The beautiful names of God, much used in popular devotion. There are ninety-nine beautiful names altogether, of which seventy are found in the Qur'ān. Among them are: Al-Azīm, the great ; al-Fattāh, the Opener, who opens the truth to men; al-Ghaffār, the forgiving one, who manifests men's good qualities and veils their bad qualities; al-Mu'izz, the giver of strength; al-Mudill, the one who leads astray; al-Kabīr, the grand one; al-Rahmān, the merciful; al-Hakīm, the wise; al-Wahhāb, he who gives freely; al-Qahhār, the Victorious; al-Latif, the kindly; al-Quddūr, the holy; al-Awwal wa-l-Ākhir, the first and last.

Īmān

Faith, consisting in conviction as to the truth of Islamic doctrine and belief.

Dīn

Ritual acts and moral obligations enjoined upon the Muslim, including the observance of prayer at the prescribed times.

'Abd

The status of man as the servant of God, commonly used in Muslim names, e.g. 'Abdullah.

Sabr

The virtues of fortitude and patience advocated in the Qur'ān. 'Allāh is with those that are patient' (Qur'ān 2.153).

Allāhu-Akbar

'God is great', the words which preface the formal prayers of Islam, and so commonly heard wherever Muslims pray aloud.

'Īsā

The word used in the Qur'ān for Jesus. The origin of this use of 'Īsā is uncertain, since it corresponds to the Old Testament name Esau rather than to Joshua, from which Jesus is derived.

Sharī'ah

The word literally means 'the path'. It is used to describe the sacred law of Islam, derived from the Qur'ān, the Sunnah, and (in some traditions) Ijmā. It indicates the close connection that exists in Islam between law and religion. Illegal and sinful actions are often the same. Sharī'ah was not fully developed until the eighth or ninth century.

Sunnah

Standard of behaviour. The word refers especially to Muhammad's sunnah, being that which he laid down by word or action, or even by the tacit approval of others.

Ijmā

A consensus of opinion among Muslims as to Islamic faith or practice. It is assumed that such a consensus will not contradict the Qur'ān.

Fatwā

Usually delivered by a Muftī, a person especially well versed in Sharī'ah, Fatwā is a legal opninon which establishes a precedent.

Ijtihād

The literal meaning is 'enterprise'. Ijtihād is a corollary of Ijmā, being the effort of the Muslim community to develop correct Islamic responses to new situations. It is regarded as a matter for experts in law and theology. A different view of the development of law and doctrine is found in Shī'ah (see Imām, p. 108).

Jā'hiliyyah

The 'days of ignorance', from which true islam frees a person. The word is used to describe the times before Muhammad and the Qur'ān.

Nifāq

'Hypocrisy'. A sham Islamic faith.

Ikhlās

Religious sincerity.

Falāh Prosperity
Tawfīq Well-being

These describe the proximate goals of Islam in this life

Rasūl

An apostle or messenger. When applied to Muhammad it is written with a definite article – al-Rasūl.

Hadīth

'Reporting', or news of what Muhammad did. This is a tradition which supplements the Qur'ān. As time went by circumstances arose which were not directly provided for in the Qur'ān, and Hadīth is a body of tradition which seeks to provide guidance for such circumstances. Hadīth refers to an oral tradition of Muhammad's teaching and practice. The traditions are said to have been transmitted through a series of authorities back to the companions of Muhammad. Discussion of the value of these traditions has been carried on at length, and has led to the production of many biographical works. The Shī'ah have their own Hadīth.

Ummah

The Muslim community or people, although the word is sometimes used in the Qur'ān to refer to Christians and Jews.

Muwālī

Clients, or non-Arab Muslims in the period of the Umayyad dynasty, when non-Arab converts to Islam had to become 'clients' of an Arab tribe.

Dār al-Islam

The house of Islam; those who belonged or converted to Islamic faith during the centuries of expansion.

Dār al-Harb

The house of war, or of non-Islam; those who resisted, physically or spiritually, the Islamic expansion.

Dhimmi

The tolerated minority within Islamic society who were not Muslim. The name usually applied to Jews and Christians living within a Muslim society. They were allowed to practise their religion, but not to propagate it. They had to pay a special tax, and lived under certain restrictions, such as not being allowed to build a house higher than those of their Muslim neighbours.

Jinn

An angelic being or spirit (from whose name the word genie is taken). The Jinns reflected popular religious ideas. They were regarded as workers of mischief or as helpers.

al-Rajīm

The name literally means 'the stoned one'. It is used of a person who is accursed (and so in some cases subject to stoning) and is commonly used of Satan.

23 Religious duties

Five Pillars of Islam
The fundamental duties (dīn) of Islam.

Shahādah
The first of the five pillars is the confession of faith: 'There is no god but Allāh, and Muhammad is his messenger.'

Salāt
The second pillar is the daily prayers, which are performed with rhythmic prostration and facing in the direction of Mecca.

Salāt al-Fajr
The dawn prayer

Salāt al-Zuhr
The noon prayer

Salāt al-'Asr
The late afternoon prayer

Salāt al-Maghrib
The evening prayer, performed immediately before sunset.

Salāt al-'Ishā
The last prayer of the day, before retiring to sleep.

Raka-āt
The sequence of the prayers and physical movements in Salāt.

Mosque
The word comes from 'masjid', or 'place of prostration'. The mosque is the Muslim place of worship. Whilst some will observe some of the times of prayer in the mosque, this is not necessary for the performance of Salāt, which may be observed wherever a Muslim happens to be. There is usually at least one public act of worship each week, held on

a Friday between noon and three in the afternoon. Mosques vary greatly in size and construction, from buildings of great splendour to humble shelters. The part reserved for worship contains very little furniture, since the worshippers sit, kneel, and prostrate themselves on the floor. Most mosques have a courtyard around or outside them containing a place for ablutions before prayer.

Wudū

Ablutions before prayer.

Mihrāb

A niche in the wall of the mosque indicating the direction of Mecca, towards which the Muslim directs his prayer.

Minaret

The tower of the mosque, from which the call to prayer is offered.

Muezzin

The person who calls the faithful to prayer. In many large mosques nowadays the call to prayer will be conveyed by amplifying equipment.

Zakāt

Almsgiving is the third of the five pillars of Islam. To give alms is regarded not simply as a charitable act but as a basic duty in sharing wealth among the Muslim brotherhood. The zakāt has traditionally been a form of obligatory giving, often a fixed percentage paid through official channels.

Sadaqāt

Voluntary giving, in addition to zakāt.

Saum

Fasting, which is the fourth of the five pillars.

Ramadān

All Muslims should fast from sunrise to sunset during the month of Ramadān. Exceptions are made for some (e.g. pregnant women, nursing mothers, and travellers) but these should make up the time of fasting at a later date.

'Īd al-Fitr

The feast which marks the end of Ramadān. This is an occasion for public worship, and for the exchange of gifts.

Hajj

The fifth pillar is the pilgrimage, or Hajj. Ideally, all Muslims should make a pilgrimage to Mecca at least once during their lifetime. In practice, of course, only some are able to do this. The best pilgrimage is one undertaken during the month of Dhū-al-Hijjah.

Ī'd al-Adhā

The pilgrim festival, although its celebration is not confined to pilgrims, and it is one of the ways in which those who cannot travel to Mecca experience some share in Hajj. 'Īd al-Adhā, also known as Bairam, is one of the main holidays of the Muslim world.

Ihrām

An act of sanctification, undertaken by pilgrims when approaching Mecca. At this point the pilgrim dons the white clothing worn by all Muslims on Hajj. The word denotes both the clothing and the state of mind in which the pilgrims should be while wearing it.

Labbaika

An expression uttered by pilgrims in front of the Ka'bah in Mecca, meaning 'Here am I before you, God'.

24 Mysticism

Sūfis

Sūfism is a movement of mysticism within Islam, and is found within both the Sunni and Shī'ah branches. It had its origins in the eighth century CE, and was initially a reaction against the worldliness of the Umayyad leadership. An ascetic movement began among Muslims, probably influenced by Syrian Christians and Nestorians. The name sūf (wool) was taken from the coarse woollen garments worn by Christian ascetics. At times the sūfis were looked upon with disfavour by the orthodox, but the movement was eventually domesticated. The sūfis sought to spiritualize Islamic concepts (e.g. in attempting to transcend the fast of Ramadān by sūfi asceticism). In their practice of dhikr they used the constant repetition of words (e.g. Allāhu, Allāhu) to develop trance-like states. (See Dhikr, p. 111).

Rābi'ah (Rābi'ah al-'Adawiyyah)
A woman who was a celebrated mystic and saint, and one of the early sūfis of Baghdad. She lived from 717 until 801, led a very ascetic life, and taught that union with God could be achieved through a love which took no account of rewards or punishments.

Hasan al-Basrī
Another early (eighth-century) mystic.

al-Hallāj
A tenth-century sūfi of extreme views, who taught that in the unitive state of mystical ecstasy man is so at one with God that the God-man distinction ceases to hold. He regarded Jesus as a perfect example of glorified humanity. Some of his views seemed close to pantheism, such as the poem which contains the line: 'I am he whom I love, and he whom I love is I'. His claim that 'I am the truth' was taken to be a claim to divinity, and he was crucified as a heretic in 922.

Abū Sa'īd
A Persian mystic, who died in 1049. He took an extreme view of the way in which sūfi mysticism could abrogate the need to make normal Muslim observances, and dissuaded his followers from making the pilgrimage to Mecca.

al-Ghazālī (Abū Hamīd al-Ghazālī)
Born in north-east Persia, al-Ghazālī is the best known of sūfi theologians. He had a brilliant career as student and teacher, becoming a professor of theology and law at a college in Baghdad. In 1096 he resigned his teaching post and left home in order to pursue a spiritual quest. He became a sūfi, and wrote books which largely succeeded in reconciling sūfi mysticism with Muslim orthodoxy. Perhaps his greatest book was 'The Revival of the Religious Sciences'.

Jalāl al Dīn Rūmī (1207–1273)
A Persian sūfi poet, and the founder of the Mawlawiyyah order.

Mawlawiyyah

The first of the sūfi orders, founded by Jalāl al Dīn Rūmī. It was a movement in whose devotion music and dancing played a large part. Members were later sometimes referred to as whirling dervishes.

Fanā'

The extinguishing of self-centredness and self-desire which was one of the aims of the sūfis.

Baqā'

A state of unity, in which the sūfi is said to be conscious of his oneness with God.

Khānqah (Zāwiyah or tekke)

An organized centre of sūfis. These cells of devotional life acted as means of promoting sūfi ideas among ordinary people, and they also served as centres of medical aid and hospitality.

Awliyā

There was great popular attraction in the sūfi idea of saints. The awliyā were 'friends of God', and were regarded as being in a line of succession of people who have succeeded in penetrating the divine mysteries. It was thought that to be in the presence of such a person was to capture something of his aura of holiness. There were many popular stories of these saints, who were sometimes credited with remarkable powers, such as levitation.

Barakah

The divine power or blessedness possessed by a saint.

Shaykh
Pīr

These were titles given to the spiritual directors of sūfis.

Faqīr

The word literally means 'poor brother', and was a name given to sūfi followers who accepted the guidance of a shaykh.

Darwish (Dervish)

The Persian equivalent of Faqīr. The Darwīshes developed ecstatic dancing as a method of cultivating trance-like states.

25 Reform movements

Wahhābi

A movement which developed in Arabia in the eighteenth century. Founded by Abū al-Wahhāb, it brought a conservative emphasis to the Islam of Arabia. The Wahhābis were critical of many aspects of popular religion, including visits to the tombs of the saints and celebrations of Muhammad's birthday. They sought a rigorous application of Islamic law, and regarded the Qur'ān and Sunnah as the only necessary authorities. Religious renewal was associated with political action. The fortunes of the movement waned during the nineteenth century, but there has been a recovery in Saudi Arabia this century, and Wahhābi influence is responsible in large measure for the rigorous attitudes of modern Saudi Arabia.

Babism

A movement founded by Sayyid Alī Muhammad, who was born in 1819 in Persia. He adopted the title of 'Bab', or 'Gate', and claimed that he superseded Muhammad as the prophet of God. He was declared insane, imprisoned, and eventually executed. But the movement continued to grow. After Sayyid's death the movement split into two groups, the largest of which was led by Baha-Allāh (1817–92). This part of the movement became the Baha'i. It claims to be based upon a new scripture, the Kitab Akdas or 'Most Holy Book'. Most Baha'i followers are still to be found in Iran, although the movement has some following in Europe and the USA.

Muslim Brethren (Al-Ikhwān al-Muslimūn)

A conservative Islamic movement in Egypt, founded by Hasan al-Bannā in 1927. Emphasis was placed upon the Qur'ān as the proper basis for the life of society. The Muslim Brethren also engaged in charitable work of various kinds. Hasan al-Bannā was assassinated in 1949. The movement was dissolved in Egypt in 1954.

Jamā'at-i-Islāmi

A movement of conservative reform in Pakistan comparable to the

Muslim Brethren in Egypt. Led by Sayyid Abūl-'Ala al-Mawdūdī, the Jamā'at pressed for the government of Pakistan in accordance with Islamic law.

Muhammad 'Abduh

An Egyptian Muslim reformer who lived from 1849 until 1905. He wished to develop an Islam purged of medieval superstition and adaptable to modern thought. He had considerable influence upon modern Egyptian Islamic thinking.

---

26 Islam in India

Sind

Sind, on the north-western borders of India, was conquered by Arab Muslims in the eighth century CE, the most eastward movement in the rapid expansion of Islam under the Umayyad dynasty. Between 711 and 713 CE. Muhammad ibn Qasim led his troops as far as the river Indus, and established an Arab administration centred on Multan, in what is now Pakistan. This limited conquest did not have great political significance for India at the time, but it did have important consequences in the transmission of Indian knowledge in mathematics, medicine, astrology and other fields to the rest of the Muslim world and thence to Europe.

Rājput

The Rājputs claimed to be ancient Kshatriyas, but in fact were mainly descendants of central Asian tribes. They crossed the North-West Frontier in the fifth and sixth centuries CE as invaders, and in due course they were admitted into the Hindu fold. For this purpose they were provided with genealogies which fitted into the Hindu caste system. In the Purānas there is a legend which tells of Paraśurāma destroying the Kshatriyas at the request of the Brāhmins. The land was then left unprotected and so the gods produced four 'fire-born' groups on Mount

Abu, in Rājputāna. This is taken to be an allegorical account of how the Rājputs were initiated into Hinduism. The Rājputs were a warlike people, with a strong sense of chivalry and great group loyalty.

Jaipāl

A Rājput king who ruled in the Punjāb until his defeat by Mahmūd in 1001. He enlisted the aid of other Rājput princes in trying to resist the Muslim invaders.

Sabuktigin

Sabuktigin was a Turkish slave who won his freedom and established a kingdom for himself at Ghazni in Afghanistan. In 986 he made his first raid into India. In 991 he defeated the Rājputs at Peshawar, and occupied the town. He built roads to the Indian frontier which were subsequently used by Mahmūd. Sabuktigin died in 997.

Mahmūd

The son of Sabuktigin, Mahmūd carried on the tradition of raiding India each year and returning home to Afghanistan with his booty. In 1001 Mahmūd inflicted a disastrous defeat on Jaipāl. He gradually penetrated further into India, and in 1018 he took Mathura. Mahmūd's most famous exploit was his raid on the great Somnath temple at Kathiawar, in Gujarāt.

Ghazni

A city in Afghanistan, Ghaznī was the capital of Sabuktigin and Mahmūd and succeeding Sultans. They were eventually supplanted by the Muslims of Ghūr, who became the next threat to the people of India.

Muhammad Ghūri (Ghori)

An Afghanistan Muslim, Muhammad Ghūri had been placed in charge of Ghaznī by his brother, the Sultan of Ghūr. He raided India, and in 1191 was defeated by Prithvīrāj. He returned the following year and defeated Prithvīrāj at Kurukshetra. This was a decisive battle, after which the Muslims penetrated further eastwards until, in 1199, they reached Bihar.

Qutab ud-din Aibak

Muhammad Ghūri's general, who later became the first Sultan of Delhi. He had been a slave, and the dynasty he founded was known as that of the 'slave-kings'. It was also known as the Turko-Afghan period, and lasted until 1290. Aibak died in 1210.

Iltutmish

A Turkish slave who had been purchased by Qutab ud-dīn, Iltutmish eventually became governor of Badaun, and was married to a daughter of Qutab ud-dīn. He became Sultan in 1210 or 1211. He rapidly consolidated his position, defeating a number of rivals. About 1229 the Caliph of Baghdad confirmed his rights to 'all land and sea which he had conquered', and so established Iltutmish's rights in the eyes of the Islamic world to be the 'Great Sultan' of Delhi and the Sind. He strengthened the power of the Turkish Sultanate, and is regarded as the greatest of the early rulers, up to 1290.

'Alā ud-dīn Khaljī

The Sultan of Delhi, 1296–1316, who seized the throne after murdering his uncle, the previous Sultan. He defeated the remnants of the Rājput armies and stamped out the vestiges of Hindu rule in North India.

Kafur (Malik Naib)

A general of 'Alā ud-dīn Khaljī who raided South India in 1310 and 1311 and penetrated as far south as Ramaswaram.

Muhammad ibn Tughlaq (Taglah)

Sultan of Delhi from 1325 until 1351, he was a fanatical Muslim. There were many rebellions during his reign, and much blood was shed.

Vijayanagar

The Hindu empire of South India which preserved independence from the Muslims from 1335 until 1565. It provided an important sanctuary for Hindu religion and culture at a time when Hindus in the North were subjugated by the Muslims.

Firoz Shāh

Sultan of Delhi from 1351 until 1388. Firoz built many new cities, and improved the economy. But he was intolerant in matters of religion, destroying many temples and erecting mosques in their places.

Tīmūr the Lame (Tamerlane)

A Bārlas Turk who invaded India after the death of Firoz Shāh and caused great havoc and destruction in 1398 and 1399. Tīmūr did not remain in India, but his attack ensured the final collapse of the Tughlaq dynasty.

The Lodīs

After a confused period of weak government at the beginning of the fifteenth century, the Lodī dynasty began with the accession to the throne of Delhi of Bahlūl Lodī in 1451. The Lodīs were an Afghan tribe. Bahlūl was a strong and vigorous ruler who began to build again the fortunes of the Delhi Sultanate.

Sikandar Lodī

Sikandar Lodī was the second of the Lodī emperors and his reign (1489–1517) was later regarded as a golden age.

Ibrāhīm Lodī

The son of Sikandar, Ibrāhīm was emperor from 1517 until 1526. He did not share the good qualities or success of his father. During his reign there were continual revolts, and this unrest paved the way for the Mughal invasion.

Mughal (Mughul, Moghul)

The Mughal rulers of India from 1526 until 1858. Their government, culture, and architecture have left a lasting impression on India.

Zahir ud-dīn Muhammad (Bābur)

A king of Kabul, his nickname Bābur means 'the tiger'. On his father's side he was descended from Tīmūr. In 1525 Bābur invaded India and took Lahore. The following year he moved on to the plains and defeated Ibrāhīm Lodī at Pānipet. He occupied Āgra and Delhi, and declared himself Sultan.

Hamāyūn

The son of Bābur, he succeeded his father in 1530 and was emperor until 1540 and again from 1555 until 1556. In 1540 a rival, Sher Shāh, seized the throne, to be followed in 1545 by Islam Shāh, who died in 1554.

Akbar

Akbar, the son of Hamāyūn, was born in 1542, and was undisputed emperor from 1562 until 1605. He is commonly recognized as the greatest of the Mughal emperors. Akbar had broad religious sympathies. He took a number of Rājput wives, abolished the poll-tax on non-Muslims, and saw good in all religions. He had conversations with Christian priests (by this time Portuguese and other European traders, and some priests with them, had arrived in India) and also adopted some Hindu and Parsee customs. Akbar also established an elaborate and effective bureaucratic organization to administer his vast empire.

Bairam Khān

The guardian of Akbar who controlled the affairs of the empire, together with Akbar's foster-mother, in the period between 1556 and 1562.

Maham Anaga

The foster-mother of Akbar.

Adham Khān

The son of Maham.

Vakil

The title given to a prime minister in the provinces of Akbar's empire.

Diwan

The finance ministers in Akbar's administrative system.

Bakshi

A paymaster.

Sadr

An officer in charge of religious affairs.

Sabas

The provinces of Akbar's empire. There were twelve provinces, each ruled by a nobleman or a member of the royal family. Sabas were divided into districts and the districts into smaller units.

Subadar

The name given to the governor of a province. Later the name was used of a rank in the Indian army.

Jahāngīr

Prince Salīm, a son of Akbar, succeeded his father in 1605 in spite of a popular uprising in favour of Khusru, the eldest son. Salīm took the title of Jahāngīr, or 'world-holder'. Jahāngīr continued contacts with Christians and Europeans, although he lacked the deep philosophical sympathies of his father. He opposed the Sikhs, and during his reign the fifth Sikh Guru, Arjan, was put to death on Jahāngīr's orders. Jahāngīr died in 1627.

Shāh Jahān

The next Mughal emperor bore the name Khurram, but took the title Shāh Jahān, or 'emperor of the world'. He was a devout Muslim, and ordered the destruction of many Hindu temples and some churches. Today he is chiefly remembered as the builder of the Tāj Mahal, a mausoleum erected in memory of his favourite wife, Mumtāz Mahal.

Aurangzeb

During the lifetime of Shāh Jahān two of his sons, Aurangzeb and Dārā Shikh, fought each other for the succession. Aurangzeb won and became emperor in 1658. He held his father captive until Shāh Jahān's death in 1666. Aurangzeb was a strict Muslim and went further than his father in his opposition to other religions. He had some great temples and Hindu holy places destroyed, and his iconoclasm was the cause of rebellions among the Rājputs and Marāthas. He also opposed the Sikhs, and was responsible for the death of Guru Tegh Bahādur. In 1680 he reintroduced the poll-tax on unbelievers. Aurangzeb died in 1707.

Bahādur Shāh

The name of Aurangzeb's son and successor, who died in 1712. This was the beginning of a long but steady period of decline in the Mughal empire. Bahādur Shāh was also the name of the last Mughal emperor who was deposed after the Indian Mutiny of 1857. He was deported to Rangoon in 1858, and he died there in 1862. Although the British assumed control of Delhi and most of India in 1803, the Mughal Emperor retained his title and at least some theoretical powers until the incorporation of India into the British Empire in 1858.

Mirzā Ghulām Ahmad (1839–1908)

He was the leader of a movement of renewal in Indian Islam. The movement, the Ahmadiyyah, wished to emphasize the claims of Islam and to combat Christianity in an area of India where Christian missionaries were active.

Ahmadiyyah

A movement which began in Lahore under the leadership of Mirzā Ghulām Ahmad. After Partition the centre of the movement moved to Rabwah, in Pakistan. The Ahmadiyyah opposed the traditional Muslim view of Christ as a prophet who will return at the end of time, and introduced a novel piece of teaching about Christ. They assert that Christ did not die on the cross, but only swooned. Later he was revived, and made his way to Kashmir. They claim that he died near Śrinagar, and that his tomb may still be seen there.

Muslim League

The Muslim League was founded in 1906 to express the political aspirations of Indian Muslims and their determination not to be swamped by a Hindu majority. One of the great leaders of the Muslim League was Muhammad Iqbāl (1873–1935), who was primarily a poet, and is now regarded by many as the national poet of Pakistan. He was an early advocate of a separate State for Muslims in the Indian sub-continent after Independence.

Muhammad Ali (1879–1930)

He was one of the original members of the Muslim League. He was eager to preserve Muslim culture and language, which he feared would be swamped in a united India dominated by Hindus. In 1913 he persuaded Ali Jinnāh (who became the founder of Pakistan) to join the League. It was due largely to the pressure exerted by the Muslim League that when India became independent in 1947 the sub-continent was partitioned and the Muslim State of Pakistan created.

Bibliography

Kenneth Cragg, *The Call of the Minaret*, Oxford University Press 1956
—— *The Event of the Qur'an*, Allen & Unwin 1971
—— *Islam and the Muslim*, Open University 1977
N. J. Dawood (trs.), *The Koran*, Penguin 1956
A. Guillaume, *Islam*, Penguin 1954
P. Holt, A. K. S. Lambton and B. Lewis (eds.), *The Cambridge History of Islam*, 2 vols., Cambridge University Press 1970
S. M. Ikram, *Muslim Civilization in India*, Columbia University Press 1964
B. Lewis (ed.), *Islam – From the Prophet Muhammad to the Capture of Constantinople*, 2 vols., Macmillan 1976
R. C. Majumdar, H. C. Raychaudhuri and K. Datta, *An Advanced History of India*, 2nd ed., Macmillan 1950
H. G. Rawlinson, *India, A Short Cultural History* (1937), Cresset Press 1965
R. M. Savory, *Introduction to Islamic Civilization*, Cambridge University Press 1976
W. Montgomery Watt, *The Majesty that was Islam*, Sidgwick & Jackson and Praeger, New York 1974

27 Sikhism

Sikh religion arose in North-West India at the end of the fifteenth century CE. The geographical centre of the Sikhs has always been in the Punjāb, along the borders of modern India and Pakistan and close to the passes through which visitors and invaders have traditionally entered India. There are two main consequences of this location in an area where many peoples have met and mixed. One is that the Sikhs are generally a physically well-endowed people; the other is that they have not become introverted. They have been, and remain, an adventurous people readily able to adapt to change.

The early leaders of the Sikhs were closely associated with Hindu bhakti movements, and Sikh devotional life has reflected the fervour and vitality of that tradition. The early Sikh movement was influenced by the presence of Islam in India and deliberately sought to find common ground between Hindus and Muslims. The first Guru, Nanak, used both Hindu and Muslim names for God. He taught that God is personal, beyond human comprehension, yet seeking the salvation of men. He emphasized the unity of God, and said that the forms by which men describe God tend to be misleading.

Sikh religion developed its distinctive forms over a period of 200 years, during which time the Sikhs were led and taught by a succession of Gurus. The Guru is thought of as a human being especially endowed to be the mouthpiece of God, and so the ten historical Gurus are held in great reverence. But they are not believed to have been divine. In spite of the great importance of the Gurus for Sikh religion, Sikhism has opposed doctrines of avatāras and incarnations, and holds that there are no intermediaries between man and God. At the death of the last Guru, Gobind Singh, it was declared that the scriptures of the Sikhs would in future be the spiritual preceptor of the community, and the Guru Granth Sahib took over the role of the human Gurus. Another vital development during the time of Gobind Singh was the formation of the Khālsā, a community of committed Sikhs who accepted the full obligations of

Sikh religion and the responsibility of fearlessly declaring their allegiance.

As Sikhism developed it came into conflict with the Muslim rulers of India. Some of its leaders, or Gurus, met their death during periods of persecution instigated by the Mughal rulers. This experience of persecution transformed the previously peaceful Sikhs into a militant community. Militant attitudes have been associated with the Sikhs ever since, and today many Sikhs in India are to be found in the armed services.

Their outgoing nature and their determination to stand up for their beliefs have made the Sikhs (who constitute less than two per cent of India's population) much more influential than their numbers would warrant. The adventurous nature of the Sikhs has been exemplified in their willingness to travel, and Sikhs are to be found in all parts of India and far beyond. They were among the earliest voluntary emigrants from India in modern times. In the early years of this century some Sikhs began a movement of migration to Canada, whilst others went to eastern and southern Africa. Sikh migration to Britain began in the early 1950s, but assumed greater proportions in the 1960s. There are today more Sikhs than Hindus in Britain.

Traditional social customs of the Sikhs have forbidden smoking, the cutting of the hair of males, and the eating of meat slaughtered in the Muslim fashion. Many Sikhs, especially those who have migrated outside the Punjāb, tend to take a liberal view of the food customs, although the prohibitions on cutting hair and smoking are more generally observed.

Sikh

A Punjābi word which is probably related to the Sanskrit 'Sishya', meaning disciple, although some suggest that it may derive from a Pali word meaning 'the elect'.

Punjāb (Panjāb)

The name means 'Land of the Five Rivers', and is the Sikh homeland, in North-West India. The position of the Punjāb, on the route between Afghanistan, the North-West Frontier, and the plains of India has made it a corridor along which most invaders of India have passed and has ensured that the inhabitants of the Punjāb have been in regular contact with the world beyond India.

Kabīr

A Hindu brought up by a Muslim family in the holy Hindu city of Varanāsi, Kabīr at first followed the trade of a weaver. He lived from

1440 until 1518 and was a disciple of Rāmānanda, a great figure in the bhakti movements of North India in the fourteenth century (see p. 35). Kabīr pioneered a devotional movement which combined elements of Islam with Hinduism. He deliberately used both 'Rām' and 'Allāh' as names of God, and his followers included some Muslims as well as Hindus. He opposed the caste system and the use of images in worship. After his death his teaching was carried on by the Kabīrpanthis. Nānak followed Kabīr as a member of the same devotional movement, and so Kabīr is regarded as in some ways a forerunner of the Sikh religion.

The Ten Gurus

Sikh history began with the first Guru, Nānak. The Sikhs had ten great leaders, or Gurus, whose work spanned two centuries, from 1496 to 1699. During this period most of the distinctive features of Sikh religion were formulated. The idea of the Guru is important, for he is regarded not simply as a teacher, but as one who is especially empowered to make God known. In Sikhism the word 'Guru' is also used of God.

Guru Nānak (1469–1539)

Nānak was born near Lahore. His life spanned the end of the Lodī dynasty and the beginnings of the Mughal Empire. He was influenced by Kabīr, by sūfism, and by Hindu bhakti movements. He is said to have had a profound religious experience at the age of thirty, and to have left his wife and two sons to become a wandering teacher. Although a Hindu, Nānak rejected some aspects of Hinduism (such as the wearing of the sacred thread and other expressions of caste distinction), and sought common ground between Hindus and Muslims. He converted both Hindus and Muslims to his beliefs, and used the methods of popular devotional Hinduism to propagate his message.

Nānak taught that God is formless, but asserted the importance of calling upon the name of the true God in prayer. Although his concept of God bears the marks of Muslim influence, Nānak accepted Hindu belief in māyā and transmigration. The implicit criticism of both Hinduism and Islam in Nānak's teaching and his rejection of caste led to the development of the new religion of Sikhism.

Guru Angad (1504–1552)

The second Guru, and leader from 1539, Angad was chosen by Nānak before his death in preference to his own sons. Angad encouraged the organization of the Sikhs into a tightly-knit community, and at his death he chose Amar Dās as his successor.

Guru Amar Dās (1479–1574)

The third Guru, from 1552 until 1574. Amar Dās reformed the ceremonies used at birth and marriage, replacing Brāhmin rites with specifically Sikh ones. He insisted that visitors should eat with the disciples, so that caste distinctions could not be observed, and he organized a system of parishes among the Sikhs. He collected the writings of his predecessors and added his own, thus forming the main source for the later compilation of the Ādi Granth.

Guru Rām Dās (1534–1581)

The son-in-law of Amar Dās, and the fourth Guru. Rām Dās promoted missionary activities among the Sikhs. In 1577 he founded the city of Rāmdāspur, now called Amritsar.

Guru Arjan Dev (1563–1606)

The fifth Guru, Arjan was a poet, philosopher, and a great organizer who played a major part in the establishment of the Sikh religion. He compiled the first authoritative canon of scripture (the Ādi Granth), and built the Golden Temple (Harimandir) at Amritsar. He suffered, with many other Sikhs, from persecution at the hands of the Mughal Empire, and died under torture which had been ordered by Jahāngīr.

Guru Hargobind (1595–1644)

The sixth Guru, and only eleven years of age when he succeeded Arjan. He began the trend away from the early pacific attitudes of the Sikhs and towards a more militant response to persecution. Hargobind was imprisoned by Jahāngīr at Gwalior for a number of years. The conflict with Mughals continued after Jahāngīr was succeeded by Shah Jahān in 1627.

Guru Hari Rai (1630–1661)

Hari Rai, the seventh Guru, spent most of his period of leadership away from the centres of Sikh loyalty because of Muslim persecution.

Guru Hari Krishan (Hari Kishen (1656–1664)

The eighth Guru was made leader at the age of five, and died when only eight years old.

Guru Tegh Bahādur (1621–1675)

During the period of office of the ninth Guru there was much opposition from Aurangzeb. Tegh Bahādur was eventually arrested and taken to Delhi in chains. He refused to renounce his Sikh faith and accept Islam, and was beheaded at Chandni Chowk, in Delhi, in November 1675.

Guru Gobind Singh (1666–1708)

The tenth and final Guru. Gobind Singh was determined to resist the Mughals more effectively, and he fought several battles against them. He formed the Khālsā with the intention of encouraging the Sikhs to be open about their religious commitment and to defend their faith vigorously. It was during his time that 'Singh' was adopted as a surname for Sikhs, and the canon of scripture was finalized. Just before his death Gobind Singh abolished the succession of Gurus, and proclaimed that in future the scriptures (Granth Sahib) would be the spiritual guide of the Sikhs.

Khālsā

The community of Sikhs formed by Guru Gobind Singh on the day of Baisākhī (mid-April) 1699, at Ānandpur. The Khālsā was intended to be a militant movement to resist the oppression of Sikhs and to further the ideals of Sikhism. Those entering the Khālsā were bidden to reject discrimination on grounds of caste, to shun superstition and idolatry, and to believe in the one true God. The Khālsā has remained an important institution, marking the full commitment of a Sikh to religion and community. But not all members of the Sikh community necessarily become members of the Khālsā.

Panj Pyare (Panch Piare)

'The Five Beloved'. When Guru Gobind Singh initiated the Khālsā, he is said to have asked the assembled company for a volunteer who would give his life for the Sikh cause. When one came forward, Gobind Singh led him into a tent, from which the crowd heard the swish of a sword-stroke and assumed that the man had been killed. The Guru called for a second volunteer, with whom the process was repeated, and then a third, fourth, and fifth. When all five had disappeared Gobind Singh drew back the covering and revealed five living disciples and five headless goats. The five disciples became known as the Panj Pyare, and typify the courage and commitment demanded by the Khālsā.

The Five Ks

The visible marks worn or carried by the Sikh. These originated with the formation of the Khālsā, and made the Sikhs clearly identifiable to one another and to their enemies. Part of the intention of the Ks was to strengthen the determination of Sikhs to withstand opposition and also, it is said, to prevent non-Sikhs being caught up in persecution through mistaken identity. The five Ks are:

Kesh
Uncut hair. The Sikh male normally allows his hair to grow long, and for this reason wears a turban, which has itself become an outward symbol of the Sikh.

Kanghā
A comb, worn in the hair.

Kach (Kachha)
Short pants, or knee-length breeches, worn instead of the long flowing robes of the Hindu and Muslim.

Kirpān
A sword or dagger as a symbol of resistance to evil.

Karā
A steel bracelet, worn on the wrist as a symbol of the unity and omnipresence of God.

Amrit
Sugared water, stirred with a sword at initiation into the Khālsā. Amrit is also the nectar of immortality.

Ādi Granth (Granth Sahib)
Ādi means 'first' and 'Granth' means 'writings'. The Sikh scriptures, which took their final form during the time of Guru Gobind Singh, are also known as Guru Granth Sahib. After the death of Gobind Singh the scriptures came to be regarded as the eternal and spiritual Guru.

Janam Sākhis
These are hagiographic accounts of the life of Guru Nānak. The words mean 'birth evidences', and the writings provide an account of the life of Nānak as seen by the eye of faith. They do not present his life in chronological order, and like the gospels they are not primarily written as straightforward biography or history. The Janam Sākhis are important, and widely used, in modern Sikhism.

Bhai Gurdas Bhāllā
A nephew of Amar Dās who acted as amanuensis for Arjan during

the compilation of the Granth. He also wrote poems which are approved for recital in Gurdwārās and are regarded as a guide to the interpretation of the Ādi Granth.

Japji

A poem, attributed to Guru Nānak, contained in the Guru Granth Sahib. It begins: 'God is one. He is the true name.' The Japji is said to summarize the teaching of Guru Nānak.

Hukam

The will of God, or the divine order by which God has created and controls the world.

Śabad (Śabd)

The 'word' of God, or the divine revelation, by whatever means transmitted. Śabad may be known through the teaching of the Gurus or the Granth Sahib or the world of nature or in mystical experiences.

Nām

The concept of the 'name' of God and the repetition of God's name are important in Sikhism. Sikhs are encouraged to meditate on the name of God, which is regarded as a revelation of the being of God. God is said to be the true name (Sat Nām), a description which is to be distinguished from personal names (Rāma, Vishnu, Śīva, etc.) used of God.

Nām Japan

The repetition of the divine name in order to appropriate spiritual benefits and transform the personality. The use of nām japan is in some ways similar to the Hindu use of mantras.

Nām Simaran

Calling to mind the divine name.

Sahaj

Realizing the presence of God, or the state of mystical union with God.

Five forces of weakness

Kām	Lust (the Sanskrit Kāma)
Krodh	Anger
Lobh	Greed or avarice
Moha	Love of material things
Ahankārā	Selfishness or pride

Khands

In the teaching of Guru Nānak these are the five stages on the road to spiritual perfection.

Dharam Khand

A recognition of basic religious values, and an acceptance of cause and effect in the religious life. Only he who recognizes that this is God's world can expect to progress morally or spiritually.

Gyān Khand (Jnān Khand)

The stage of knowledge at which one has the perception to recognize spiritual qualities.

Saram Khand

The third stage, that of effort. The disciple must apply his perception in strenuous effort.

Karam Khand

There are various interpretations of the meaning of karam khand in Guru Nānak's teaching. One interpretation is to regard karam as grace bestowed upon the believer; another is to take karam to be the equivalent of karma, and so to refer to the consequences of past actions: and a third possibility is that karam relates to karma in the sense of being the action which accompanies effort.

Sach Khand

The fifth and final stage is that of truth. At this stage the believer attains unity with the divine.

—

Man

A word which is the Punjābi equivalent of the Sanskrit manas, or mind. In Guru Nānak's teaching it means an inner sense by which truth may be apprehended. The word is also used for the self, or ātman.

Haumai

Self-interest or self-centredness. The pride and self-assertion which cause people to ignore the divine order.

Gurumukh

The person in whom the Guru's (or God's) voice is heard.

Manmukh

The person in whom only the voice of self-interest is heard.

Gurdwārā

Literally, 'The Gateway of the Guru'. The Gurdwārā is the Sikh temple, used regularly for worship but also a centre of social activity. In addition to a large area for worship, a Gurdwārā also has smaller rooms which can be used for preparing and eating food.

Sangat

The congregation of Sikhs which gathers for worship in the Gurdwārā.

Karah Prasād

The symbolic and sacred food distributed at the conclusion of the service in the Gurdwārā, and received by everybody present. The Prasād is a sign of God's benevolence.

Gurū-kā Langar

'The Guru's kitchen'. This is a separate room in the Gurdwārā to which the congregation go after the service in order to share a common meal. It is Sikh practice to share food with any, including visitors, who attend the Gurdwārā, and this relates to the desire to obliterate caste distinctions.

Niśān Sāhib

The flag flown at the Gurdwārā. It is usually a saffron colour (the holy colour of India). It bears an emblem of two scimitars in the centre of which is a circle bisected by a two-edged sword.

Ardās

A formal prayer at the Gurdwārā service. The phrase 'Waheguru' – 'wonderful Lord' – is repeated throughout this prayer.

Ānand

The prayer of thanksgiving.

Bhajan

A hymn or religious song. Sikh worship is congregational, and includes the singing of bhajans as well as readings from the Guru Granth Sahib, prayer, and a sermon.

Sat Śri Akal

The phrase, which means 'God is truth', is a common Sikh greeting.

Singh

A suffix, meaning 'lion', commonly added to the personal name of a male Sikh. The use of Singh in Sikh names began in the time of Guru Gobind Singh, and is part of the deliberate self-identification of Sikhs which developed at that time.

Kaur

A suffix, meaning 'princess', added to the name of a female Sikh.

Sardār

A form of address for Sikh men.

Sardarni

A form of address for Sikh women.

Jats

Peasant cultivators who assumed leadership early in the history of the Khālsā, and who have remained an important element in Sikh history ever since. Although caste distinctions are not normally allowed to obtrude in the Gurdwārā the Sikhs, like other Indian people, are still much influenced by caste and community groups. The Jats function as a caste group among the Sikhs.

Kesadhāris (Keshdhāris)

Unshaven Sikhs, who adopt the full forms of Sikhism and adhere to the demands made upon the Khālsā.

Sahajdhāris

Sikhs who do not adopt the full forms of Sikhism, but claim to adhere to the teaching of Guru Nānak.

Udāsis

Members of the Sahajdhāris group whose loyalties were partly Hindu. The Udāsīs controlled the administration of the Gurdwāras for a long time.

Ranjit Singh (1780–1839)

A Sikh leader who defeated the Pathāns and Afghans, and established Sikh military dominance in the Punjāb.

Nāmdhāris

A nineteenth-century reform movement among the Sikhs, most of whose members belong to the Rāmgarhia caste. Their first leader was Rām Singh (1816–1884). Their practice includes austere living, strict vegetarianism, and an emphasis upon prayer. They adopt an unorthodox view of the Guru, holding to a living guru and so rejecting the full authority of the Guru Granth Sahib.

Singh Sabhā

A movement which began in the 1870s, the Singh Sabhā has been concerned with the renewal of the Sikh religion and the resistance of conversions to Hinduism and Christianity. The Sabhā established many schools and colleges.

Akali Dal

A Sikh political party, the Akali Dal campaigned for full Sikh control of Gurdwārās in the Punjab, many of which were controlled by Udāsīs. The campaign came to a successful conclusion with the passing of the Sikh Gurdwārās Act. The Akali Dal also worked for the establishment of a separate Sikh State in the Punjāb.

Bibliography

Gopal Singh, *The Religion of the Sikhs*, Asia Publishing House, Bombay 1971
Harbas Singh, *Guru Nānak and Origins of the Sikh Faith*, Asia Publishing House, Bombay 1969
W. H. McLeod, *Guru Nānak and the Sikh Religion*, Clarendon Press 1968
R. C. Majumdar, H. C. Raychaudhuri and K. Datta, *An Advanced History of India*, 2nd ed., Macmillan 1950
Terry Thomas, *Sikhism: The Voice of the Guru*, Open University 1978

28 Modern Hinduism

The Mughal Empire began to disintegrate from the early eighteenth century. Europeans were increasingly part of the Indian scene, and although ostensibly they were present on the sub-continent as traders they exercised increasing political control. From 1803 the Mughal Empire was placed under British 'protection', although India did not officially become part of the British Empire until 1858.

Hindu religion and culture, much weakened by centuries of Muslim dominance, had to face the criticisms implicit in Western scientific thought and in the work of Christian missionaries. Modern education was introduced from the West and inevitably provided a vehicle for Western and Christian ideas.

At first Hinduism reacted defensively. Hindus participated in movements to rid India of undesirable social practices, such as child marriage and the burning of widows on their husbands' funeral pyres. Attempts were made to reform Hinduism in the light of Christian influence. But towards the end of the nineteenth century the mood changed. Hindus became more self-confident and increasingly resentful of Western criticism. Westerners began to appreciate the richness of Hindu culture and religion as the great Orientalists translated works from Sanskrit and other Indian languages (the series 'Sacred Books of the East', edited by Max Muller, began to appear in 1879). The new mood of confidence among Hindus at the end of the century coincided with nationalist aspirations and with increasing criticisms of Western values.

The first half of the twentieth century was marked by the pursuit of political independence, with an accompanying desire to find a genuinely Indian selfhood, and by continuing attempts on the part of Indian philosophers to assert the value of Hinduism in a world context and against the exclusive claims of other religions. Popular religion continued its vigorous life in the villages and towns, largely untouched by changes in the world beyond.

Rām Mohan Roy (1722–1833)

A Bengali reformer of Hinduism; a man of great intellectual ability and a brilliant linguist. He served in the Bengal Civil Service and in that career rose as high as it was then possible for an Indian to go. At the age of forty-two he retired in order to devote himself to writing and to social and religious matters.

He opposed idolatry in popular Hinduism, and advocated reform in the light of Western scientific and rational thought. He welcomed the humanitarian message of Christianity and expressed his appreciation of Christian ethical teaching in a book called *The Precepts of Jesus, the Guide to Peace and Happiness*. The book emphasized the moral teaching of Jesus whilst rejecting the supernatural claims of Christianity. *The Precepts of Jesus* was vigorously attacked by some Christian missionaries, and this led to something of a reaction on Roy's part. He began the publication of the *Brahmanical Magazine* in oder to defend Hinduism against the attacks of missionaries. Rām Mohan Roy was involved in many attempts at social reform, and it was largely due to his efforts that the burning of widows was made illegal in 1829.

Roy died in Bristol whilst on a visit to England to represent the titular Mughal Emperor in Delhi before the British Parliament. He was later called 'The Father of Modern India', and was the first in a line of great nineteenth-century reformers of Hinduism.

Brāhmo Samāj

A society founded by Rām Mohan Roy in 1828 to express the ideas of a Hinduism purged of superstitious accretions. The Samāj was basically rationalistic in its outlook, and reflected Christian and Western influence. The first 'church' of the Samāj was opened in 1830. Services were held which included readings from the Upanishads, sermons, and the singing of theistic hymns. The Brāhmo Samāj played a significant part in the reform of Hinduism, although it was a society of intellectuals and had no popular appeal.

Debendranāth Tagore (1817–1905)

Debendranāth was a Brāhmin who became the second great leader of the Samāj. He at first maintained that the Vedas taught pure theism, and even sent four young men to Varanāsi to study the Vedas in order to establish their theistic nature. When the study did not confirm this view Debendranāth gave up his belief in the inerrancy of the Vedas and rested Brāhmo interpretation of scripture upon intuition.

Keshab Chāndra Sen (1838–1884)

He was one of the great leaders of the Samāj, joining the movement in 1857. He was an active social reformer, and campaigned for such issues as the remarriage of widows and education for women. In 1865 Keshab broke with Debendranāth Tagore and became the leader of a separate branch of the Samāj called the Brāhmo Samāj of India. Debendranāth's group was then known as the Ādi, or original, Samāj. A further split occurred in 1878 when Keshab, who had long supported the raising of the minimum age for marriage, sanctioned the marriage of his thirteen-year-old daughter to a young Indian prince. Many of his followers were incensed at this, and left him to form the Sādhāran (General) Brāhmo Samāj. Keshab appears to have been much affected by meetings towards the end of his life with Rāmakrishna, and particularly by the latter's teaching that 'all religions are one'. In 1879 Keshab established 'the Church of the New Dispensation', which he claimed fulfilled the teaching of both Old and New Testaments and incorporated what was best in other religions. The 'church' held services which were similar to Christian services, and used symbols taken from Christianity, Islam, and Hinduism. But this movement did not have popular appeal, and little of it survived Keshab's death in 1884.

One of the most significant aspects of Keshab's teaching was his acceptance of a doctrine of Christ which was very close to orthodox Christianity. This has attracted fresh attention in recent years as Indian Christian theologians have attempted to formulate a fresh understanding of the 'Indian Christ'.

Prārthanā Samāj

The Brāhmo Samāj was largely a Bengali movement. But interest in reform was not confined to that part of the country, and in 1867 the Prārthanā Samāj was formed by members of a former organization called the Paramahmasa Samāj. The four main objects of the Prār-thanā Samāj were: to break down caste distinctions; to introduce the marriage of widows; to encourage the emanicpation of women; and to campaign for the abolition of child-marriage.

Mahādev Govind Rānade (1842–1901)

Rānade was a Judge of the Bombay High Court and a founder of the Indian National Congress. He was an active social reformer, and a leader of the Prārthanā Samāj.

Dayānanda Sarasvati (1824–1883)

(Also known as Swāmi Dayānanda.) He was born into a Brāhmin family in Gujarāt, an area then largely untouched by British influence. He had an orthodox upbringing, becoming proficient in Sanskrit and in a knowledge of the Hindu scriptures. He revolted against the practice of using idols, or images, in worship, and based his teaching upon the Vedas, which he claimed were not polytheistic. He also claimed to be able to find the doctrines of karma and transmigration in the Vedas. Dayānanda was the founder of the Ārya Samāj.

Ārya Samāj

Founded in Bombay in 1875, the main purpose of the Ārya Samāj was to recall Hindus to a purified version of their own faith and to combat the appeal of Christianity and Islam. The Ārya Samāj has been particularly influential in North-West India, and has been more closely connected with Hinduism and the lives of ordinary people than has the Brāhmo Samāj. The Ārya Samāj is still in existence, and continues to promote Hindu nationalism and to oppose foreign and non-Hindu influences in India.

Theosophical Society

The Society was founded in New York in 1875 by Madam Blavatsky and Colonel Olcott. Originally the Society rested upon strange claims of occult powers and contact with spiritual 'masters' in Tibet. But theosophy also professed admiration for all things Indian, and led a number of Westerners to India not to preach Western values but to express support for Hinduism. In this way the Society had a not inconsiderable influence on the growing self-confidence of Hinduism at the end of the nineteenth and beginning of the twentieth centuries.

Annie Besant (1847–1933)

An English Fabian and social reformer, Annie Besant went to India with the Theosophical Society and became an enthusiastic advocate of Hinduism. She also promoted the cause of Indian nationalism, and in 1917 became the fifth and last British President of the Indian National Congress.

Rāmakrishna (1836–1886)

Born Gadadhar Chatterji, of a simple village family in Bengal, Rāmakrishna became a temple priest at Dakshineswar, near Calcutta. He had a number of intense spiritual experiences which led people to regard him as a great mystic, and he is acknowledged to have been one of the greatest spiritual figures of nineteenth-century India. He combined fervent devotional religion, directed towards 'the Mother' or Kāli, with theoretical acceptance of Advaita Vedānta (see p. 43). Although a largely uneducated man, Rāmakrishna had a gift of perceptive teaching which was couched in homely terms, and many people visited Dakshineswar to see and hear him. His emphasis was upon personal experience as the touchstone of true religion, and he made much of the assertion that 'all religions are one'. Shortly before his death some of his followers began to worship him as an avatāra (see p. 28).

Vivekananda (1863–1902)

Vivekananda's original name was Narendra Nath. His father was a barrister, and he had a Western-style education at Presidency College and the Scottish Church College, Calcutta. As a student he attended the Brāhmo Samāj, but was disenchanted with what he regarded as the lack of genuine personal religious experience among the leaders of the Samāj. He became a follower of Rāmakrishna, and assumed the leadership of Rāmakrishna's disciples after his death in 1886. In 1897 he was instrumental in founding the Rāmakrishna Mission, which became a most effective agent of social service and religious teaching in India, and also established centres in Europe and the USA for the propagation of Hindu teaching. Vivekananda visited the World Parliament of Religions in Chicago in 1893 and proved to be a highly successful apologist for Hinduism abroad. He criticized Christian and Western ideas and attitudes and asserted the claims of Hinduism, and especially of Advaita Vedānta, to be the most perfect expression of religion. He did much to restore the self-confidence of Hindus in their own religion and culture.

Aurobindo (1872–1950)

Aurobindo Ghose, often referred to as Śrī Aurobindo, was born in Calcutta. His education and early experience was entirely Westernized. He was sent to a convent school at the age of five, and when only seven years old was sent to England where he remained until he was twenty. After his return to India in 1893 he became involved in the work of revolutionary organizations and the nationalist movement generally. He served a term of imprisonment, and in 1910, when under threat of arrest, he fled from British India and went to live in Pondicherry, which was then under French rule. There Aurobindo took up the study and practice of Yoga. He established the Aurobindo Āshram, and remained in Pondicherry until his death.

Aurobindo wrote many books in which he put forward an original interpretation of Indian philosophy. He attempted to bring together a number of Western ideas, particularly on evolution, with the main stream of Indian thought. The Aurobindo Āshram at Pondicherry, and more recently the new town of Auroville adjacent to it, have become centres for people from different parts of India and the world to come together to study and follow the teaching of Aurobindo. So far the movement has been largely one of intellectuals and has not yet had much popular appeal in India.

Rabindranāth Tagore (1861–1941)

The son of Debendranāth, Rabīndranāth Tagore was a great poet and writer in Bengali and English. Perhaps his best-known work is 'Gītānjali'. Tagore won the Nobel Prize for Literature in 1913. He was a noted internationalist and humanist. He rejected many traditional Hindu beliefs, and had little sympathy with the politics of the independence movement or the philosophy of Mahatma Gāndhi.

Sarvepalli Rādhakrishnan (1888–1975)

Born in 1888 at Tiruttani in South India, Rādhakrishnan was educated in Christian institutions, at Voorhees College, Vellore, and Madras Christian College. He had a brilliant academic career, becoming Professor of Philosophy first at the University of Mysore and later at Calcutta University. He became Spalding Professor of Eastern Religion and Ethics at Oxford. His books include *Indian Philosophy, The Hindu View of Life, An Idealist View of Life*, and *Eastern Religions and Western Thought*.

Rādhakrishnan claimed that there is an essential unity in all the great religions of the world; that mysticism is the most important element in religion; and that Hinduism is particularly well suited to act as a meeting place for religions because of its doctrinal tolerance. Dr Rādhakrishnan followed his academic career by serving as Vice-President and then President (1962–67) of India.

Mahatma Gāndhi (1869–1948)

Mohandes Karamchand Gāndhi is regarded by many as the greatest man India has produced this century or, indeed, in modern times. His name is usually written either with Mahatma (great soul) before it or with the suffix 'ji' (Gāndhiji), which is also a mark of great respect.

Gāndhiji was born into a Vaishnava Hindu family in Gujarāt, an area affected less than most by Western influence, and a centre of Jaina religion. He had an undistinguished career at school, and after a failure at a local college he was sent to England in 1888 to study law. He returned to India in 1891, having qualified, but not practised, as a barrister. He had difficulty in obtaining employment in India, and in 1893 went to South Africa to represent the legal interests of an Indian firm there. Events caused him to stay in South Africa until 1915, and it was in leading Indians in South Africa in their attempts to combat discrimination and obtain civil rights that he forged his personal philosophy and his technique of non-violent resistance.

On his return to India he became active in the Independence

movement. During the nineteen-twenties he led members of the Indian National Congress in programmes of non-co-operation, and in the nineteen-thirties he launched widespread campaigns of civil disobedience. He adopted a simple life-style, identifying himself with the poor of India. He came to be regarded by many as a great religious figure and a saint as well as a political leader.

A devout Hindu, Gāndhi nevertheless took a liberal view of some aspects of Hinduism, and campaigned vigorously against untouchability. He also acknowledged the influence upon him of other religions, including Christianity.

When Independence was gained in 1947 Gāndhiji refused to accept any public office. He was greatly distressed by the communal rioting between Hindus and Muslims which accompanied the partition of India and Pakistan, and he toured the country appealing for peace and for tolerance between different religious communities. Mahatma Gāndhi was assassinated by a Hindu fanatic in 1948.

Some important words in Gāndhian thought

Ahimsā

Gāndhiji adapted the teaching on ahimsā, or non-violence, found in Jaina, Hindu and Buddhist thought and made it an important part of his religious and political philosophy.

Satyagraha

Literally the force, or struggle, of truth, satyagraha was a name coined for the movement of non-violent resistance which Gāndhiji developed in South Africa. He emphasized that satyagraha is an active and positive struggle for truth and justice, and so preferred this new word to 'pacificism'. The inspiration of satyagraha came from the doctrine of ahimsā and also from such sources as the writing of Tolstoi and the Sermon on the Mount. Mahatma Gāndhi developed satyagraha into an effective political weapon. His technique has since been copied by others working for civil rights, and most notably by Martin Luther King.

Sarvodaya

The service of all. Sarvodaya is a social and economic theory, the aim of which is to create a society free from conflict of class or property. Sarvodaya rejects both capitalism and communism. It teaches that all property belongs to God and to the community, and that duty rather than right should determine the relation of the individual to the community. In formulating his ideas of sarvodaya Gāndhiji was much influenced by his reading of Ruskin's *Unto This Last*.

Swadeshi

The love of one's neighbourhood. The idea of swadeshi played an important part in Gāndhiji's struggle for Indian independence. In economic terms swadeshi implies a preference for goods and articles produced by one's immediate neighbour. and rejects foreign goods in favour of national products. In social terms, it implies service to the immediate neighbourhood. And in ethical and religious terms it teaches the rejection of communal hatred and the acceptance of the religious tradition into which one is born.

Harijan

Literally 'children of God', the expression was used by Mahatma Gāndhi of the untouchables in his campaign for their betterment.

Bibliography

P. D. Bishop, *The Life and Teaching of Sri Ramakrishna*, Unpublished M.A. Thesis, University of Manchester 1966
—— *The Rāja Yoga of Vivekananda and the Integral Yoga of Aurobindo*, Unpublished Ph.D. Thesis, University of London 1973
W. T. de Bary (ed.), *Sources of Indian Tradition*, vol. 2, Columbia University Press 1964
J. N. Farquhar, *Modern Religious Movements in India*, Macmillan 1915
Swami Gambhirananda, *History of the Ramakrishna Math and Mission*, Advaita Ashrama, Calcutta 1957
The Life of Swami Vivekananda, by Eastern and Western Disciples, Advaita Ashrama, Calcutta 1960
Shriman Narayan (ed.), *The Selected Works of Mahatma Gandhi*, Navajivan Publishing House, Ahmedabad 1968
A. B. Purani, *The Life of Sri Aurobindo*, Sri Aurobindo Ashram, Pondicherry 1964
Swami Saradananda, *Sri Ramakrishna, the Great Master*, Sri Ramakrishna Math. Madras 1952

Index

Bold figures indicate places where the entry appears in bold type in the text